Making Purpose Work

Making Purpose Work

The Challenge of Growing Ourselves and Our Companies

Franchee Harmon

HPH Publishing
Chicago, IL

First edition: April 2006

Copyright © 2005 Franchee Harmon

The moral right of the author has been asserted.

Cover Illustration by Illustration Works
Photographer: Boris Lyubner
Copyright Illustration Works, Inc/Getty Images

HPH Publishing, 333 West North Avenue, Chicago, IL 60610

Publisher's Cataloging-in-Publication Data

Harmon, Franchee. D.
    Making purpose work : the challenge of growing ourselves and
our companies / Franchee Harmon.
    p. cm.
    Includes bibliographical references and index.
    ISBN 0-9776281-0-8
    ISBN 13 9780977628100

1. Success in business. 2. Employee motivation. 3. Self-perception. 4.
Performance--Psychological aspects. 5. Organizational effectiveness.
6. Self-management (Psychology). 7. Neuropsychology. I. Title.

HF5549.5.M63 H368 2006
658.31419--dc22
2005937712

Printed in Canada

*In loving memory of
my dad,
Henry P. Harmon*

Contents

Making Purpose Work

CHAPTER 1

Business and Purpose

Why Purpose Matters

This book is about continual change, evolution, and growth: talents required to make purpose work. Yet, it is equally about the natural limitations our minds place on us to resist this, which is why for most of us purpose doesn't work. This is not, however, a book about spirituality, religion, or any belief system that has to do with any God or religion. It is a book about how ordinary people like you and me, can make purpose— our desire to find relevant contextual meaning in our lives—work for us. And by working for us, help us to better understand the private and personal wars we constantly wage with ourselves as we strive to grow and evolve individually and organizationally.

I started writing this book for you. But I ended up writing for me: to help in my desire to make purpose work in my life. In doing this, I'm not certain whether I will succeed or whether I will fail in the effort. In fact, whether I do or not isn't really the point. The point is, no matter what the outcome, change will occur: definitely in me, and hopefully, in you. Obviously, without this change, no matter how small or seemingly inconsequential, purpose can't work.

This fact seems so simple, so fundamental, that it hardly seems worth writing about. Yet, we all know that change is anything but simple. It is downright hard for all of us. Our mental processing systems just aren't readily structured to help us deal with change easily or naturally. It requires great effort and will to overcome the things we dislike most about ourselves and the world around us. Sometimes, it seems nearly impossible. *Making Purpose Work* explores why: why we find it difficult as human beings and why we find it difficult as organizations. But equally important, it explains what we can do about it.

Although this is a book to help me and you, it is not a self-help book. It is a business book. But unlike other business books, it wasn't written for a particular management group or type of functional specialist or any other narrowly defined section of an organization. It was written for everyone in the organization. Because change, evolution, and growth impacts all of us. And we all contribute to an organization's ability to achieve it. Without the ability to change, evolve and grow, just like individuals, organizations will never achieve their purpose. Needless to say, as the tragedy of Hurricane Katrina in New Orleans highlighted, when our businesses, governments, and educational institutions fail in their goal to change, evolve, and grow, we all shoulder the consequences. So, we all share the responsibility to learn. This book also explains what actions we can take to share in that responsibility.

With that said, let's begin to learn how.

Why Purpose Matters to Business—The Theory

Purpose is shorthand for meaning. And basically, that is exactly what it does. It gives meaning to customers, employees, and other relevant stakeholders of the firm. If these stakeholders can relate to this meaning (and that is not a given), actions productive to the firm occur. These actions, generated by emotions, involve five characteristics of purpose: self-identity, instincts, expectations, fear, and unity. In the individual, these five characteristics generate action that:

- Draws on instincts to create goal-directed results;
- Fuels expectations to create successful outcomes;
- Encourages facing fears and inspires self-motivation;
- Forms principles and values we use to work together; and
- Helps us understand who we are (define ourselves).

In other words, when purpose translates into contextual meaning that stakeholders can identify with, businesses get great results. When that meaning is less understood, we get less than great results. Actually, we get unhappy employees, poor products and services, unreliable suppliers, an ineffective Board, and the list goes on and on. Given the list of possible unproductive actions, it should be clear that we all succeed together and fail together, despite what our inequitable reward structures suggest.

These results, productive and unproductive, occur because at an organizational level, the five characteristics combine to create the structure of the firm. They continue to operate at an individual level but a new layer of complexity exists as the individuals within the firm organize to work together as a unit. Within this structure, the five characteristics re-form to generate productive action that:

- Utilizes our instincts to deliver competencies and capabilities;
- Harnesses our expectations of the future by creating products and services;
- Addresses our fears and tries to inspire our motivation through strategies;
- Institutionalizes principles and values by creating ideologies, rules, and regulations; and
- Defines us organizationally through processes, procedures, structures, and systems.

The pictorial below illustrates the layering of the five characteristics as they arrange themselves individually and organizationally to achieve purpose.

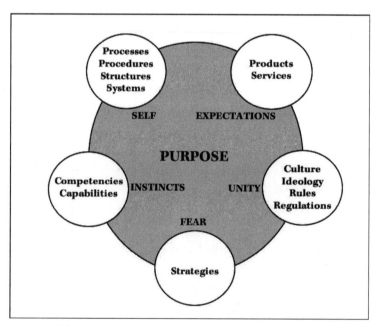

Why Purpose Matters to Business—The Reality

In theory, that is how purpose works. And it has worked in reality. The problem is, it doesn't work very often. For the remainder of this chapter, we will discover some of the conditions under which purpose does work. To demonstrate this, we will consider Sony. At its peak Sony, in spite of their current reality of not being able to make purpose work, historically serves as a sterling example of how well it does work. I'd like you to consider their story.

Many know of Sony's phoenix-like rise to greatness. Like others of their era, they began life at a time when the value of life had been reduced to nothing. This was a time of war. Yet, this period, this occasion, this epoch, created not a sense of despair but a sense of purpose. Harnessed by emotions, against the backdrop of extraordinary devastation, one of the most successful companies ever was formed.

Pretend for a moment that you are Masaru Ibuka, a cofounder of Sony. After many years, World War II was finally at an end: a war that tore the world, and families, and lives, apart. As far as one could see across the city of Tokyo, devastation lay all around, a constant reminder of defeat. How does one survive when all that is familiar, stable, and secure is gone? We create meaning, which is exactly what Ibuka did.

In his eyes there was much to build on. There was hope, 1600 yen, 20 eager colleagues, and a small, dismal work area on the 3rd floor of the bombed-out Shirokiya Department Store. And importantly, they had passion, a vague vision, and values. This was enough. It was enough because the latter three items utilized characteristics of purpose that helped the company create meaning and, using this meaning, achieve phenomenal growth.

When Sony's small team began, they had little of anything. There were many weeks when only a single yam or a handful of toasted soybeans was the meal for lunch. But as Akio Morita, the other cofounder of Sony, recalls, when he first saw Ibuka after the war, "there was enthusiasm on Ibuka's face, and he and his employees were happy." Despite their conditions, emotional energy took charge to help steer them through an uncertain journey. Along that journey, the five characteristics of purpose were used in many different ways.

During the war, Ibuka had run his own company, Nihon Sokuteiki or Japan Precision Instrument Company. Although the firm had plenty of work to adequately sustain the business, Ibuka did not feel professionally satisfied. At the war's end, he and seven colleagues decided to return to war-torn Tokyo and start over. Ibuka was an idealist. He was not afraid to dream and to seek realization of his dreams. But his dreams were not simply for his own sake; he was deeply concerned about the needs of others.

Perhaps, this is why Sony was built on the Philosophy of Mu, or "Nothingness." Even though Ibuka had worked with his men and perhaps understood their wants and needs, he did not seek to prescribe what the purpose of the business should be by defining for the group exactly "who they were" and "what they sought to become." This is clear from a statement contained in the Tokyo Tsushin Kogyo (the founding name of the company) Prospectus, which states: "...Not anyone, but those with similar resolve have naturally come together to embark on this new mission with the rebirth of Japan after the war. We felt no need to discuss how to prepare ourselves for such an embarkment. Based on a common understanding we had developed over time, our ship sailed off naturally." Free of prescription, they worked together to continuously discover their way based on "nothingness." And through "nothingness," Ibuka and Morita allowed every individual in Sony to define for himself and herself their place in the company, from the highest-ranking executive to lowest-level factory worker. Shigeru Kobayashi, the manager for Sony's Atsugi Plant from 1961 to 1969, explains the Philosophy of Mu, or "Nothingness," in *Creative Management*:

> "'Nothingness' does not mean that the company is to be managed on the basis of whim from day-to-day or that no fundamental principles are involved. It does mean that without being hampered by our own and others' fixed ideas, we are [free] to observe honestly both the subjective and the objective aspects of conditions as they appear to be at various times, set our goals accordingly, and establish means of achieving those goals in a spirit of complete open-mindedness. It means that even if the conclusions reached in this manner should prove to diverge widely from generally accepted thinking—or our own thinking up to that point—we will implement them with courage and fervor."

In the spirit of "nothingness," the firm built the foundation upon which they would work together collectively to discover the answers to "who they were" and "what they sought to become." This situation of realization is important, as an individual's primary source of meaning is derived from their belief in self. Without this freedom of development, an individual's need to continually preserve self-identity is suppressed as autonomous seeking is deprived. It is through seeking that we explore and learn. Without new learning, neural connectors , which contribute to creating aspects of the self, deteriorate over time. Thus, "nothingness" was important to helping the group continually discover, through seeking, ways to sustain themselves, economically and psychologically.

Their initial explorations focused on practical ideas such as sweetened bean paste soup and making slide rules as well as not-so-practical ones like building a miniature golf course. Finally, they settled on the ideas of a rice cooker and a heating pad to keep people warm. As this young team experienced, they learned, and through learning, they dreamed up new things to create. Consequently, it was in these early months of seeking, through dreaming and creating, that Ibuka formulated the company's purpose.

From the beginning, Ibuka and his cofounder Akio Morita dreamed of "a concept of a company as an innovator, a clever company that would make new high-technology products in ingenious ways." Moreover, Ibuka was determined that the company would focus on producing consumer products that were new market concepts. As Ibuka sat down to write the Prospectus for founding Tokyo Tsushin Kogyo, these matters weighed on his mind. He united these ideas eloquently in the Prospectus, laying out the company's purpose for the next forty years. The purpose in the Prospectus reads:

Purpose of Incorporation [items f-h have been omitted]

a) To establish an ideal factory (sic) that stresses a spirit of freedom and open-mindedness, and where engineers with sincere motivation can exercise their technological skills to the highest level;

b) To reconstruct Japan and to elevate the nation's culture through dynamic technological and manufacturing activities;

c) To promptly apply highly advanced technologies which were developed in various sectors during the war to common households;

d) To rapidly commercialize superior technological findings in universities and research institutions that are worthy of application in common households;

e) To bring radio communications and similar devices to common households and to promote the use of home electric appliances.

As Morita would later say in his autobiography *Made in Japan*: "We were engineers, and we had a big dream of success." Through confidence, they set their expectations high and never wavered from them. These expectations set them up for what is termed "feelings-as-evidence." When seeking confirmation of an uncertain outcome, we often consult (so to speak) our feeling to determine whether they are consistent with our belief. Consistency helps us align belief in a proposition, such as "we will be successful," with feelings, like confidence. If our feelings and believed proposition have coherency, the sensation of feeling may be treated like sensory evidence from the external environment, so that something believed propositionally and felt emotionally seems especially valid. The stronger our perceived validity, the greater our buy-in that the expectation will be realized. Sony had great expectations.

One could also say that this small, then unknown, group was fearless and highly motivated by the consequences of failure. We are all aware that the challenge of survival totally changes our situational perspective. Tragic events, such as September 11th, the War in Iraq, and Hurricane Katrina have heightened our awareness of how this need state and the reactive forces associated with it operate. Through these circumstances, we have added new words to our vocabulary like fear conditioning. Although tragic events can lead to fear conditioning that we normally associate with negative outcomes, positive conditioning outcomes are also possible when challenging survival events involve teaching us to be fearless. Looking at fear in this light, Sony's experiences helped positively condition their fear perspective. By facing threats of the unknown fearlessly, the company successfully worked through many uncertain and survival-threatening events.

An early threat to survival was their desire to produce a color tube to introduce a color TV set. After successfully entering the US television market with the Tummy Telly (a portal TV set), Sony found itself desperately behind. Nevertheless, Ibuka was determined to produce a color tube. "I could see no fun in merely copying [RCA's] excellent system," said Ibuka. Even though their delayed entry greatly disappointed their dealers, who knew they were missing a great opportunity, and hindered their financial performance, Sony stayed their course. After five years of unsuccessful efforts, the team had a concept that could possibly work but many challenges lay ahead. This trying time was recounted in *The Sony Vision.*

"Yoshida's [the engineer in charge of production] biggest problem was convincing the production staff that [it] would actually work. They had lived for more than five years with the unsuccessful Chromatron and there still lingered that sense of demoralization, the nagging feeling that, even after they had come so far, this system too would fail. Yoshida insisted this would not happen. Supported by Ibuka, who was there daily—arguing, watching, discussing progress, and problems with even the youngest engineers—the Sony Manhattan Project began to gain momentum." By having the courage to continue, despite many failures, Sony created what would come to set the standard in color tube engineering—the Sony Trinitron. For this effort, in 1973, Ibuka accepted an Emmy on behalf of the Corporation for "Outstanding Achievements in Engineering Developments."

While some might consider such risk-taking foolish, particularly given the availability of the patent, which all other industry players used, we will see in later chapters that threatening situations make greater use of our emotion-driven abilities, when compared to simple process-oriented tasks. Ibuka saw no challenge in process-oriented imitation of RCA, who held the industry-dependent color tube patent. And somehow, he instinctively knew he would not get the best from his engineering team without a worthy challenge. Using courage in the face of adversity, which the company had set as an expectation, they rose to the occasion and exceeded their lofty objective.

Leveraging emotion-driven abilities was successful because it enabled Sony's work teams to use their instincts to craft goal-directed outcomes. This self-organizing, operational style was evident throughout the organization, but it was best exemplified in Ibuka's guidance to management hires. Noiro Ohga, who is now retired from Sony's board of directors, was on his way to a promising career as an opera baritone when Ibuka and Morita persuaded him to join the Sony team. On his hiring, he had no prior technical or business training. Yet, he rose to hold wide-ranging responsibilities within the firm. After only five years, he became a board member. Like many Sony executives, his position was created on the basis of "finding something for him to do." And this is exactly what the company did. Having hired a person, not filled a position, they found the most challenging jobs possible. While this might seem like "setting people up to fail," actually, the reverse occurred. As one man put it: "I never worked so hard in my life. I never knew what hidden abilities were inside me until I came to Sony." Without situations that challenge our understanding so that we utilize emotion-driven abilities to craft goal-directed outcomes, most of us never do.

Unfortunately, yet another benefit is lost with emotion-deficient actions. Allowing individuals to utilize their situation-interpretation skills freelyto create goal-directed outcomes draws out the individual's passion that creates reverence within a closely associated group. Reverence stimulates the emotions of admiration and sympathy. These emotions are needed to establish and maintain principles and values amongst the group, by which they work together to realize their purpose.

The values of trust and loyalty were central to Sony's culture. This was achieved through reverence created as a result of motivating individuals by giving them joy in their sense of achievement, pride in what they did, recognition for their efforts, and a sense of mission. Ideas more easily verbalized than they are achieved. Yet, Sony accomplished this, not through declaration, authority, reasoning, or bribery, like most managers today, but with heartfelt sympathy and admiration. Through sincerity of purpose, reverence was achieved using non-manipulative emotional triggers. In this fashion, a two-way balance was achieved to maintain values that bound the individual and company together. Nick Lyons captures this sentiment artfully in *The Sony Vision*:

> "Pointing to his heart and his head: 'So much of what Sony means to us is here and here. It's difficult to describe. We all feel different and we know we are treated differently; we do business differently. We are given

responsibility and encouragement. Our opinions count. It is a feeling you get about this company. Sometimes you are afraid to say it: it sounds like it's dipped in honey. But it's here...'" (Quoting an American manager)

Each purpose characteristic that guided Sony's behavior was drawn out through emotions: happiness, confidence, fearlessness or courage, pride, and finally, sympathy and admiration. Emotion lies latent in the individual. When we're singularly focused on goals, we miss the critical actor in purpose-creation—the individual. Without the individual, the benefit of emotion is lost, and thus, the benefits of purpose are not realized. Under the leadership of Ibuka and Morita, Sony never lost sight of this.

Purpose is not about goals; it is about people and action. That action is only unleashed when the meaning needed to elicit emotion is present. Without it, there is no purpose.

When we fail to create meaning, we also fail to create belief. And as we will explore shortly, creating meaning without belief to back it up is like trying to attach paper to a wall without an adhesive. You can hang it up there, but it's not going to stick. To endure the uncertainty, pain, and often, thankless commitment required to make purpose work, meanings need belief to hold them up. How does this happen? You'll discover that in a moment.

CHAPTER 2

What's Belief Got To Do With It?

Defining Belief

Snow White is one of the world's most beloved animated features. Its imagery and liveliness brought mere cartoon characters to life on screen. It is still, 65 years after its release, a work of genius. A work the world almost never came to know. If it were not for belief, Snow White would have remained on the animators' drawing boards, a figment of Walt Disney's vivid imagination.

One evening after working hours, Walt Disney called his animators together to discuss a new project: *Snow White and the Seven Dwarfs*. The project was to be one of their greatest animation efforts to date. The characters had to come to life and seem alive on screen. Mechanical movements that characterized previous cartoons would be eliminated and it would be a full-length feature film, not a cartoon short, as were their earlier projects. It would push their creative talents to the limit. All this excited Walt Disney, and it was obvious in the meeting. In the tradition of Walt, he acted out each character, demonstrating its personality, features, and human qualities, including the sound of their voices and their mannerisms. It was an Academy Award-winning performance that mesmerized his animators. But Walt's older brother Roy was not convinced. He was concerned about cost and public interest.

The Disneys saved quite a nice nest egg over 10 years of producing cartoon shorts. Little risk was involved as they were paid when the short was completed. For this project, they would have to finance it themselves, taking the risk of success or failure at the box office. Walt estimated that the budget for Snow White would run half a million dollars, almost their entire savings. Through persuasion, the project proceeded. Over the course of the production, the budget mushroomed to a final bill, exceeding many times the original estimate. Each time funds were exhausted, Roy went to Bank of America for more money. During that era, Bank of America had little interest in placing loan money at risk; they were not gamblers. Although the Disneys had built a good relationship with their bank, this project severely tested the strength of that commitment.

Walt Disney was also a perfectionist. Over the two years that it took to complete the film, Bank of America continued to loan them money. Still, no one at the bank had any idea what the final product would look like. Pre-screening before completion was unacceptable in Walt Disney's eyes. Yet, the pressure to get a final round of funding was crucial. According to one account of this story, Roy eventually managed to get his brother to provide a pre-screening to Joseph Rosenberg, Bank of America's representative in Los Angeles. With many pieces of the plot still on the drawing table, at best, pencil sketches and unfinished clips were all the Disney's could show for their hard work. Walt's intimate relationship with the story brought each missing section of the plot to life. He even sang songs that had not yet been dubbed into the film. It was a virtuoso performance of spontaneous ad-libbing. Rosenberg made no comment when the screening ended. Assuming the worst, Walt walked him out to his car.

After opening the door, he looked at Walt and said: "That thing [*Snow White*] is going to make a hatful of money." Fortunately for the Disneys, who were deeply in debt, it made many hatfuls of money through the belief of Walt in his dream and his animators and Joe Rosenberg's belief that Walt Disney would complete it.

Have you ever considered what life would be like without belief? Belief was crucial for Walt Disney. It is through belief that he became one of the most prolific imaginers of the 20th century. Without belief, there would be no Disney. Actually, without belief, there would not be much of anything. Consider the possibility for a moment. Would love have any meaning if we couldn't believe in our marital partners or significant others? Could we instill in our children the motivation to succeed if we did not believe in them? Would we still think the world was flat and that the sun revolved around the earth if it were not for belief? Without belief man would never have traveled to the moon. There would be no technology. No literature, no art, no cinema, no parks, no business, no trust, and no honor. A man's word would not be his bond without belief. Nothing that man can not be certain of comes into existence without belief. It is our mental processing faculty that allows humans to act without knowing.

This is a book about sustainable achievement of individual and corporate goals through purpose. But to understand how we accomplish sustained achievement, we must understand belief. For by delving into the deepest domain of our inner selves—emotions and feelings that define our beliefs—we have the best possibility of understanding the true nature of sustainability. We also have the possibility of better understanding strategies that improve the probability of survival. This understanding can help us harness the power of belief to achieve greater benefit from productive beliefs and lessen the impact of or deter unproductive beliefs. In the world of corporate strategy, we constantly work to balance these counteracting forces to achieve purpose.

Beliefs permeate our lives. They power everything that we think and do, yet we fail to understand them or in some instances even acknowledge them. They are a part of who we are, what we think, how we act or re-act, and why we are the way we are. Like it or not, they are ever-present. Beliefs are sometimes rational and sometimes not. There can be good beliefs and bad beliefs. Still, there is belief nonetheless.

In the corporate world, whether we chose to admit it or not, there is also belief. Some companies choose to run their businesses principally on the strength of their beliefs. Others not. Some companies, very successfully, put belief above all else in guiding their strategy. However, most often, it is deemed more appropriate to go with the facts rather than to go with beliefs. Yet, is there really a difference?

It is impossible to deny that in a decision, any decision, personal or professional, that belief does not play some role in our thinking. We don't know everything about its role, but we know that belief is an important variable in the equation. In fact, when we are faced with complex decisions wrought with uncertainty, we know belief plays a critical role. Exactly how critical, we are just beginning to understand.

Part of the reason for this is that our belief and decision frameworks are intricately connected to our emotions. We are learning that we use these emotions to help us rationalize our world and to make decisions. Part of that rationalization process is triggered through the beliefs that we build up over time in our emotional sensory system. Often, we are not even aware that these emotions have come into play. Although early research is helping making these relationships clearer, more work is needed to fully understand how these complex and silent partnerships work.

Consider the act of creating a company's philosophy of purpose and its related business strategy. This is an event where information is generally complex, ambiguous, open-ended, and voluminous. At some point, executives must "see-through" this clutter to unearth a direction or vision for the company. How, when, why, and what beliefs underlie judgments in decision-making? Without perfect information, some unseen element has been used to arrive at a particular conclusion. What is it, and how has belief played a part?

We also experience these unseen forces in relation to unproductive beliefs. Studies recount how employees actively resist implementing positive change strategies they "believe" are harmful to the company. In their minds, they are acting in the company's best interest. What are these "beliefs" that drive them to hinder the potential success of a company they want to help? How can these beliefs be better understood to identify their existence and use their energy to help reinforce positive change?

These are questions central to this book. To improve our ability to make purpose work, it is crucial that we first seek to understand belief. And the reason for this is clear: beliefs, spoken or not, play a crucial unseen role in everything we do in our personal and professional lives. It becomes increasingly difficult to execute plans effectively the deeper beliefs are buried, productive or unproductive.

Without an understanding of beliefs, we diminish the levers we have available to us to motivate, support, and, if required, deter negative behaviors of those responsible for achieving the company's purpose and strategy, which is everyone in the organization.

As such, this is an exploration into belief as a lever for improved strategic execution. In some ways, it is a journey, which is itself built on belief. In other ways, it is a road that leads down many different paths, each providing small insights into the nature of the problem. From either avenue, we have a chance to critically examine our self and our role in helping to build successful purpose-driven companies. Not in relation to assigned titles, tasks, roles and responsibilities, but in relation to the complexities of who and what we are. Fundamentally, it is an examination into the complexities that drive our beliefs, for better or for worse. The hope is that we can harness this learning to realize the potential of an underutilized strategic asset: individuals.

In this chapter, we examine how meaning and belief go hand in hand. More importantly, we will discuss how particular dimensions of belief contribute to our inability to change our context of the meanings we create, for better or worse.

This examination covers the perspective of neuroscientists, social psychologists, memory scientists, and other scientific disciplines. From these insights, a definition of belief is derived that will stand for the course of this book.

As David Hume rightly pointed out, belief is such an integral dimension of what man is that we take it for granted. We are our beliefs. As such, philosophers assumed no great difficulty in explaining it. Yet, 3,000 years later, we still struggle to do so. After knowledge was defined by Plato as "justified true belief," philosophy focused on knowledge and what "justified" belief. Scarce attention was given to the nature of belief itself. David Hume was one of the few philosophers who attempted an explanation. Even he, however, expressed great difficulty in finding words that could adequately convey his meaning. In fact, he suggested that we each look to ourselves for an answer. Reflecting on this thought provides an interesting starting point for our discussion.

While writing this chapter, I was challenged by the idea that everyone knows what belief is. I asked myself: "What are you trying to say about belief that people don't already know?" After all, we all have beliefs—meaning, each of us has our own understanding as Hume noted. Let me stop right here. This is exactly the point I wish to get across to you. All you or I really know is what belief is for us individually. Now, I'd like to extend that point further. In every scientific discipline that studies belief, this situation exists: each person knows what belief means within his own discipline. So, while I know what belief is for myself, I don't always know what it is for my mother or brother or sister or best friend or anybody else. Philosophy calls this the "Other Mind" problem. We can't know what is in another person's mind, no matter how much we sense that we can because we know someone extremely well—it is not possible to know anyone *that* well. The various scientists who study belief also face this problem. All I really have to know is what my mother or others near to me believe. Fortunately, I have enough experience of my mother to generally know her beliefs, but she can surprise me. Scientists have to try to integrate the views of other scientists into a coherent theory that encompasses all their ideas about belief. So, if each of my numerous family members represented a scientific discipline, I would have to try to integrate their understanding of belief into one coherent meaning. This is not as easy as knowing what belief is for just me, or a scientist knowing what belief is just for his or her field. So, notions of belief are biased towards a self-serving worldview. To understand belief, these notions must be inner– and outer-focused to be inclusive of the many dimensions of belief.

You might find this confusing and wonder why there are so many dimensions of belief. Isn't it just related to my acknowledging something as being true and my feelings towards that truth? Well, yes and no. Let me explain.

The question of belief began in philosophy 3000 years ago. And at that time, philosophy was a discipline that delved into many other disciplines. It touched on every aspect of science as we know it today. However, as science matured, the study of philosophy became a narrow field of science that had served as the birth mother for numerous other disciplines. In the separation of philosophy into these numerous disciplines, belief was separated as well. With this separation, each discipline came to see the role of belief as a particular function of the human organism and its related definition from the perspective of that function.

We can sum it up this way: when philosophy proliferated in many disciplines of science, varying discipline-centric views of belief resulted. This fact is not lost on the *Encyclopedia Britannica* which states: "Believing is *either* an intellectual judgment or, as the 18th century Scottish Skeptic David Hume maintained, a special sort of feeling with overtones that differ from those of disbelief."

In this definition, philosophy began the tradition of thinking of beliefs as propositions of agreement—an intellectual judgment, where a proposition is a truthful statement—but there are many others. Most of us are familiar with this definition, which is generally presented in the following form:

x believes that p,

where p is replaced by some sentence expressing the proposition believed: snow is white. Most of the focus of such analysis centers on justification for x's belief that p—philosophy's offspring, cognitive scientists, followed this tradition. Their cousins, the social scientists, see belief as: "People's information about their social and non-social environment, be that information accurate or inaccurate." In this definition, belief provides information about how people construct their world. Psychoanalysts and psychologists are equally less concerned with belief justification and more concerned with the meanings behind belief and the significance to us personally. If you believe in vampires, the psychologist cares less about the truth of that belief and more about why you think the vampires will come visit you tonight. In any case, the vampires might be related to false beliefs, which memory scientists are interested in. We cannot overlook this discipline because memory and belief are closely related. Memory scientists define belief as an inclination to behave in a manner that is resistant to correction by experience. In this regard, knowledge, in contrast to belief, is a behavioral tendency that is constantly subject to corrective modification and updating by experience. So memory plays a large part in what we treat as knowledge versus what we treat as belief. Delving more deeply are the neurologists and cognitive neurologists who care about how our brains actually process belief. They focus on our neurological stimulus responses to the environment. Belief in their view is seen as the result of a number of factors rooted in our organisms and in the culture in which we have been immersed, even if such factors may be remote, and we may not be aware of them. This domain works with patients who have various mental disorders. Working to understand these disorders helps identify clues to pinpoint the neurological basis for belief. Their findings are critical to our understanding. Taken together, these self-serving worldviews from various scientific disciplines represent the many dimensions of belief. So, you've seen the nature of the beast; let's see if we can construct a whole monster rather than fragmented statements that can be attributed to it.

Considering these varying perspectives, I think belief is defined as:

> Mental catologs of emotionally-competent sensory and/or internal autonomous stimuli that help us determine truth and assess meaning. These varying sensory stimuli stubbornly plant themselves within our neural sensory processing environ and manifest their existence consciously and unconsciously in multiple ways through actions, both verbal and nonverbal.

It took a year and a half to construct that definition. Here's why. We needed to nail down the many dimensions of belief without regard to the mental phenomena addressed. This definition achieves that. Having the right belief dimensions is similar to having the right ingredients for a cake. To make a cake that achieves a desired outcome—a tasty eating experience—we need eggs, milk, flour, butter, and other appropriate ingredients. If an ingredient is missed, we spoil the cake. Until now, we hadn't identified all the ingredients necessary to provide a multi-disciplinary definition of belief. I believe we do now. And I believe this definition will help us understand the context between purpose and belief.

The belief dimensions that makeup our multi-dimensional definition are outlined here:

Dimension	Description
Catologs Stimuli	Belief stimuli tag neural markers in our sensory processing environment creating records of their existence.
Resists Updating	Markers are planted in emotional and procedural memory systems and are resistant to change through information updating as they bypass declarative (cognitive) memory
Determines Perceived Truth	Truthfulness of a concept, related to the marker, is questionable or open to varying interpretations
Assesses Meaning	Interpretations of the concept and related marker have life-or-death significance for the individual or group
Expresses Existence Consciously and Unconsciously	Markers triggering belief make their existence known consciously and unconsciously (without mental awareness)
Prompts and Provokes Action	When markers are triggered, action occurs (verbally and nonverbally) often without knowledge or awareness

Basically, belief is a sense-making faculty that acknowledges that we do not know, but we must act or react. This should not really come as a surprise to any of us. To make sense of our need to know, we use our mental and emotional processing systems to interpret stimuli that have left neural markers of their existence. Sometimes we know a marker has been left—a painful incident that led you to believe something about someone or thing. At other times, we are absolutely unaware of the existence of markers—prejudices against something or someone. We act (when necessary) on these markers based on context-situated belief. Thus, belief is a default mechanism for dealing with uncertainty and unknowns. Intuition is one of our belief-formulation vehicles. In some respects, it is a primitive mental-processing function that autonomously generates routine beliefs, with low levels of concept complexity. But our brain also uses intuition for more complex concept interpretation, such as complex mathematics and innovative idea generation of varying forms. To understand how belief allows us to act without knowing, let us begin our discussion of the many dimensions of belief.

Catologs Stimuli

If belief is sense-making faculty, how do we make sense of things? This question will frame our discussion of multi-dimensional belief. To answer it, we need to understand the nature of a concept and how humans conceptualize the varying sensory information around them. Plato's *Theory of Ideas* is useful here. In Plato's theory a form represents the fundamental essence of something, a common denominator through which many things having similar basic elements can be grouped together. Plato said that humans do this by reasoning. The sorting process that Plato communicated underlies the way we create and understand concepts. Why are most trees referred to as "trees" rather than specifically as oak, elm, palm, cherry, apple, birch, etc? It could be that we cannot specifically define enough trees to do so. Or even if we could define them, we could not recall all of their correct names. Imagine having to remember the specific name of everything that exists in the universe. The task would be daunting. Communication would be nearly impossible and understandable only by those who could agree on definitions and recall items with exacting specificity. If we didn't have the ability to categorize, life would be unmanageable. It's difficult enough simply to remember the names of people that we meet throughout our lives.

Categorization is a natural brain function that allows it to shortcut organizing and placing specific details into higher-level concepts. If we did not have this faculty, the world would become a bewildering array of specific items to which one thing could never be related to another by some common functional element. Plato's Theory of Ideas goes to the heart of this sense-making faculty in human beings. This means that our minds naturally catalog things and order them for understanding.

The sensory inputs that are encoded within our neural environment are cataloged in the same way. Each sensory input can be thought of as a marker that leaves a record of its existence. We are not always consciously aware that a marker has occurred. In technical terms, these markers are called synapses, the junction between two nerve cells. Synapses allow cells to transmit signals. When these synapses are not used, ultimately they deteriorate. Active markers remain in our memory systems and make their existence known when required.

Resists Updating

It is obvious that memory is important to learning. How well we remember and recall is constantly assessed through various forms of standardized testing used to determine intellectual ability. Through the study of memory, we know a lot about how we use short– and long-term memory. Such studies explain why, for example, we are limited to immediate recall of about five to seven items when we go to the grocer without a list. This is short-term memory in action. Conversely, we have no problem remembering the names of numerous relatives and extended relatives, their birth dates, their partners or significant others, their addresses, their phone numbers, and other minute details about them. When we do this, we use one component of long-term memory, our ability to recall facts—declarative memory.

During the past ten years, however, other distinctions of long-term memory and its varying locations within the brain have become better understood. When I hear a familiar song play that transports my thoughts to an event in my distant past, my mind is engaging experience using episodic memory. As I whiz along Lake Michigan during my first roller blade attempt, the mechanics of being able to iceskate help make acquiring that new skill seem effortless. By drawing on what is called nondeclarative (also referred to as procedural) memory, I used a skill learned previously but not applied in that particular manner before. While memory type has distinct functions in learning, its location within the brain has implications for using that learning as knowledge or belief.

This last statement may seem surprising, particularly to philosophers who have always considered knowledge and belief as essentially the same mental phenomena.

Knowledge for the philosopher is justified belief as first defined by Plato. Outside of philosophy, belief and knowledge have always been treated as differing forms of information acceptance. Belief is defined as being based on acceptance because of how we feel about something. In contrast, knowledge is defined by acceptance after considering the facts, information, or learning we have acquired about something. Where in our brain systems a marker resides, dictates whether information acceptance will be used as memory-without-knowledge, which is belief, or knowledge.

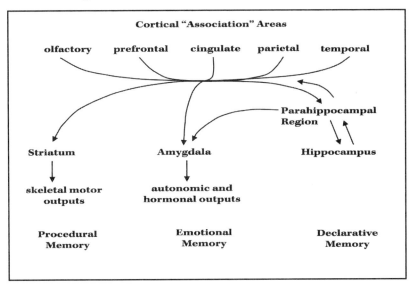

Three different brain regions address each form of memory: declarative, nondeclarative, and emotional. Declarative memory that enables knowing resides in the hippocampus. In this region, knowing is bought to consciousness and information acceptance is subject to updating through experience or explicit recall, new specific facts and instances, and mentally manipulating information about these facts. Memory-without-knowledge (belief) occurs in brain regions that feed into the hippocampus but can also process memory independently. You may already be aware of one of these systems, the amygdala. It's considered to be the home of our emotional memory. Nondeclarative memory, which I used to learn to roller blade, is housed in the striatum. Both these systems process memory unconsciously and autonomously. According to Howard Eichenbaum and J. Alexander Bodkin, authors of *Belief and Knowledge as Distinct Forms of Memory,* "belief-driven memory processing is comprehensive enough to guide complex behaviors that are high in motivation, emotion, and goal directedness. At the same time, this kind of learning occurs without introspection, investigation, or doubt." Using emotional and procedural recall, these brain systems enable memory-without-knowledge. Because belief and knowledge work in tandem, it is difficult for us to always determine which is actually in use. When belief is the driver, information-processing acceptance is resistant to updating because processing takes place outside the hippocampal knowledge structure.

Assesses Meaning

The fact that our minds resist change and treat anything as certain seems paradoxical. The world is uncertain. If we are honest about it, there are only three certainties: death, change, and the laws of nature. Few things that we can think of can be considered fixed and settled, which would make them certain. Gravity, a law of nature, falls into this category. Still, laws of nature cover a thimble-worth of human knowledge. After that we must rely on principles. This is about as exacting as scientists can get, but even here there is considerable room for doubt. Below this, uncertainty begins to creep in substantially. In spite of this, we can behave as though the world is quite certain when we choose to.

The immutable existence of uncertainty raises an interesting question. If the world is uncertain, why are we pre-wired to be able to choose to behave with certainty or not? Let's consider an example. You've decided to buy a house. After speaking to real estate agents, looking at houses, securing a mortgage deal, examining schools, and thinking about commuting issues, amongst other things, you now want to make a decision. Each variable in your decision has some degree of uncertainty. But our various mental processing faculties allow you to make either a belief-based decision using, say intuition, or to take a knowledge-based approach using, say rational thinking.

To understand choice under uncertainty, economists and social psychologists have focused on notions of risk, utility, and satisfying outcomes. However, appraisal theorist, Richard Lazarus, proposes that our need for understanding personal significance overrides these factors. Personal significance determines whether we choose to believe and act with certainty or to know and respond or not. Without personal significance, we have little need to be concerned with certainty. When relevance is ambiguous, having knowledge does not imply that we must act on it.

Individuals determine relevance through appraisal. Appraisal allows us to continually evaluate the significance of what is happening to our well-being to derive meaning. Without personal significance, knowledge is unemotional And in some respects, irrelevant. When significance impacts well-being, it is emotional and highly relevant. Hans Kreitler and Shulamith Kreitler noted in *Cognitive Orientation and Behavior* that to assess significance, individuals focus on two questions: what does it mean, and what does it mean to me and for me? From these two questions a myriad of other questions naturally emerge.

Processing these questions at a conscious level, we reason out numerous survival strategies. At the unconscious level, our bodies react to signals from various markers of memory experiences that exist. In such instances, these markers drive the appraisal process.

In the cognitive worldview without emotions, meaning did not and does not exist. There is no evaluation of how and whether what is happening is harmful or beneficial. With emotions, appraisals can be either deliberate or autonomous, depending on what is happening around us. If you were to walk out into the street and a car suddenly careened toward you, your emotions would take over directing you to freeze or move. Which option is engaged depends on the amount of reaction time available. Either way, action will occur immediately. Now let us assume that when you walk into the street, the same car is weaving recklessly. This time, however, it is one city block away. Assuming a less immediate situation, your emotions use that time to interact with your higher cognitive functions. The significance to you is assessed and various strategies for survival evaluated. As your mind had more time for your emotions to signal several parts of the brain, it did not simply rely on less sophisticated reaction strategies. Other strategies were bought into play that involved brain systems other than the amygdala, our emotional memory. Nonetheless under both circumstances, personal significance and issues of survival were the mind's first priority. When these issues are immediate and threatening the brain reacts with certainty.

Determines Truth

Once we can ascribe meaning to something, how certain we need to be about it becomes self-evident. Clearly, some things have more meaning and require more certainty than others. We can start with the love of our families and significant others as easy examples. Could we develop family bonds or committed relationships without treating unknown truth as certain? As we have just discussed, issues related to life or death require not only that we can assess certainty but that we can take action. Belief enables that. When our bodies release autonomous signals and emotions indicating certainty, we act. So while philosophers were well intentioned when they sought to limit our need to rely on this natural mental processing function, they overlooked the fundamental reason we need the ability to believe. We must be able to treat unknown truth as certain. As we stated at the start of this chapter, creation would not exist without it. And without unquestionable reactions, we place our existence in jeopardy by limiting the resoluteness of our actions.

In chapter 8, Fear, we will discuss how belief-driven processes guide motivation and goal-directedness without doubt or reflection. For now, we are going to review, at a high level, how the mind processes unknown truth using meaning to assess the relevance of uncertainty.

Let us consider again the prospect of purchasing a home. Under purely knowledge-based processing, evaluating your decision parameters is potentially long and arduous. As a first step, you will possibly want to give each variable a probability to reflect its uncertain nature. Next each variable should perhaps be weighed against other variables so that important variables are given greater significance. To ensure that uncertainty and importance is appropriately assessed, each variable would need to be researched in detail. Clearly, this process would take quite a long time to complete, and some people do choose to do this. By first engaging belief-based processing, our minds shorten this process and increase the accuracy of decision-making process. Using the markers, we derive the significance of unknown truth, such as the quality of the neighborhood school, and assess what relevance, if any, we should place on this uncertainty. Neurologist Antonio Damasio, who developed the somatic marker hypothesis, explains how it functions in *Descartes' Error*:

> "Markers force attention on the negative outcomes to which a given action may lead, and function as an automated alarm signal that says: Beware of danger ahead if you choose the option that leads to this outcome. The signal may lead you to reject, *immediately*, the negative course of action and thus make you choose among other alternatives. The automated signal protects you against future losses, without further ado, and then allows you to choose from among fewer alternatives...Somatic markers are a special instance of feelings generated from emotions. Those emotions and feelings have been connected, by learning, to predicted future outcomes of certain scenarios. When a negative marker is juxtaposed to a particular future outcome, the combination functions as an alarm bell. When a positive marker is juxtaposed instead, it becomes a beacon of incentive."

Belief-based processing provides us with guidance to move forward in our decision-making using knowledge-based processing. However, variables with truths that are questionable or potentially harmful have been identified. And equally important, their relevance as an uncertainty has been determined. By limiting our decision choices and reducing uncertainty, under some circumstances, belief helps improve the chances of achieving positive outcomes.

Expresses Existence Consciously and Unconsciously

My first job out of university was in construction. I was an engineer for the Illinois Department of Transportation ("IDOT"). This is the branch of state government responsible for design and construction of the state roadway system. As one of several inspectors, I performed evaluations and tests to ensure that contractor's construction methods were in compliance with IDOT's design and specification requirements. On one hot summer day, I was inspecting a road construction project in a southwest suburb of Chicago. The area was quite pretty. Most residents were upper middle households, and the community lies near one of the city's nicer forest preserves. I was happy to have the assignment, particularly in the midst of summer. If you have ever passed by a roadway construction project, you know that the conditions are not very nice. When the grinding machines remove the existing pavement, dust flies everywhere. For the asphalt to adhere to the resurfaced area, the temperature of the mix at delivery needs to be at least 180 degrees Fahrenheit. Add to this a day when the outside air temperature has surpassed 90 degrees Fahrenheit, and you have a very unpleasant work situation. But on this assignment, we were fortunate. The temperature that day was hot, but the shade of the trees in the preserve provided great protection from the sun and cooled down the construction area.

There is another aspect of construction work that you might have noticed as you rode along the roadway or passed a building under construction. Canteen trucks come by at regular intervals to provide food for the crews. Our team location also had a canteen vendor that visited the site regularly. Her visit on this day was no different to others, except she arrived earlier than usual. Seeing her, I decided to take an early break to get a cool drink. As I approached the stand, I could see a young man ordering something from the vendor. At first, he did not notice me. Suddenly as I moved closer, he turned, looked at me angrily and said: "What do you want nigger?"

For decades, this has been the face of prejudice. We viewed prejudiced people as angry, somehow misguided, warped individuals, who just didn't get it.

In 2001, a watershed occurred in the boardrooms of corporate America. Three African American men were named CEO of Fortune 500 companies. In a Newsweek cover story relating this noteworthy event, the following was shared about Kenneth Chenault, CEO of American Express: "Hired to plan strategy, Chenault did well toeing the company line, and was attracting attention. At the time, recalls Amy Digeso, a former AmEx personnel executive, there was a lot of buzz around the company about the exceptional newcomer. A straggler who'd heard about Chenault but had not yet met him entered a room one day and was introduced. 'My God, you're black', Digeso recalls the man saying. 'Ken said, Yes, I know.'" Richard Parsons, CEO of Time Warner, shared this story: "On one occasion in the late 1970s, Nelson Rockefeller dispatched Parsons to the Metropolitan Museum in Manhattan to negotiate a dispute. The loyal deputy arrived and presented himself to the museum's lawyers. The group ignored him, and for several minutes they kept looking at the door, apparently expecting a team of Rockefeller attorneys. 'Finally, I said, 'What are we waiting for, guys?'" Parsons recalls. They quickly looked for a way out of the awkward moment." Finally, in a Newsweek article on black women, President of Ariel Capital, Mellody Hobson, shared her story: "People come into my office all the time where I'm the president of the firm, and they give me their coat and ask me for coffee because they don't know who I am. So, I go hang up the coat, get the coffee, and then sit at the head of the table."

These are the subtle realities of stereotypes and prejudices. What we now understand is that the unconscious nature of prejudice and stereotype is inextricably linked to our cognitive processing structures. Consider again the dimensions of belief discussed earlier. The first issue is our need to categorize. This is a fundamental processing strategy that allows us to simplify our otherwise overly complex world. Next, our memory systems are designed to retain procedural and emotional stimuli to assist us in rapid and unwavering autonomous responses. Last, our minds automatically minimize information-processing effort by engaging belief-based strategies to shortcut determining context-situated meaning and its relevance. I am certain that none of the business professionals involved in the above stories would consider himself or herself prejudiced. Yet in situations where unconscious belief drove their actions, they behaved in a prejudiced manner.

In *Memory, Brain, and Beliefs,* contributors Banaji and Bhaskar, sum up the situation:

> "Social psychologists have moved from the view
> that stereotypes and prejudices reflect the warped

beliefs and preferences of distasteful individuals who threaten harmonious social existence, to the view that such processes are best considered the unhappy and even tragic outcome of the ordinary workings of human cognition. As a consequence, a fundamental interconnectedness between the cognitive processes of memory, perception, attention, categorization, and reasoning on the one hand, and the social processes of stereotyping and prejudice on other hand, became permanently established ... Our position is that all humans are implicated to varying degrees in the operation of implicit stereotypes and prejudice. The pervasiveness of such expressions has been underestimated because large portions occur outside the awareness and control of both perceivers and targets. Based on evidence of the ways in which perception, attention, categorization, and memory operate to produce biases in judgment, stereotyping and prejudice too must be viewed as the outcome of ordinary and automatic thinking and feeling."

Our conscious actions pose little problem for realizing the productive benefits belief can bestow. The problem, and it is not insignificant, lies in unearthing and addressing unconscious processes that drive many aspects of our behavior. As we think about the implication of stereotypes and prejudice for businesses, clearly, the issue of diversity and its achievability is in question. However, the problem is much deeper. Remember, we categorize everything! So when a consultant publishes a book or report stating that graduates with a 700 GMAT score, or 1400 SAT, or 3.6

GPA are the only candidates worth considering, we begin to categorize. Everyone who meets these statistics is a worthy candidate, and everyone who does not is not. We have just created a stereotype. If company performance is determined by a respected management thinker to be based on seven specific criteria, and those seven criteria become extensively used within organizations, we have again created a stereotype. We walk a very fine line between developing principles that guide us and creating situational circumstances that limit accepting things outside our contextual worldview. Principles are not certainties. As principles are continually reinforced through our procedural and emotional memory, they begin to be treated as certainties. Once principles become belief-based, the list of not acceptable versus acceptable categories begins to grow and grow. Over time, we are left with few things that are acceptable and many that are not, without mechanisms to overcome our mental resistance to alternatives. Such strategies create organizational, social, and economic stagnation that ultimately negates any productive benefit belief has to offer.

Prompts and Provokes Action

Throughout our discussion of the multi-dimensional nature of belief, we have touched on action. Action is the natural and autonomous response to our body's assessment of our well-being and survival. Keep in mind that well-being and survival relate not only to whether we remain alive and healthy. Well-being and survival relate to every idea of self that we constantly fight to maintain. This includes ideas of moral behavior, ideas of faith, ideas of constituting and organizing social groups, political systems, distribution of wealth, running economic enterprises, and the state of culture. Emotions and beliefs are the gatekeepers to unleashing action related to any of these ideas of self, survival, and well-being.

Several examples of this have been covered. At the start of this chapter, we learned how Walt Disney used belief to secure funding for Snow White. Both the survival of the firm and the survival of Walt's project rested on his ability to use belief to convince Joseph Rosenberg. It was belief that guided Walt's performance during that critical meeting. In the first chapter, we saw how Sony used belief to survive. They focused on ideas of economic determination, culture, and moral behavior to drive their actions. At a crucial point in their survival while developing the Trinitron picture tube, they harnessed belief that allowed them to push their intellectual talents to the limit, refusing to accept failure as an option. We also discussed negative actions resulting from belief: professionals whose unconscious beliefs compelled them to engage stereotypical attitudes related to roles of particular genders or ethnic groups. In all cases, belief compelled action, either verbal or nonverbal.

It seems clear as we examine the many dimensions of belief, that people and actions lie at its heart. Belief is not about goals. Without the individual, for better or worse, there is no belief. Without belief, there is no action.

It's the failure of us all to understand this reality that continues to foster the problems of stereotypes and biases. We're not immune to engaging in steroetypical/biased actions no matter what our station in life. This is clear when the recent statements of Harvard University's President, Dr. Lawrence Summers, and William Bennett, former Education Secretary, are considered.

In order of occurrence, let's discuss Dr. Summers first. In a speech during the NBER Conference on Diversifying the

Science and Engineering Workforce, Dr. Summers posited, as one of three hypotheses, that the difficulty of identifying elite female scientists may arise from "innate" differences between men and women (A complete transcript of Dr. Summers remarks can be found at *http://www.president. harvard.edu/speech/2005/nber.html*). Several months later, Mr. Bennett told a caller to his syndicated talk show: "I do know that it's true that if you wanted to reduce crime, you could—if that were your sole purpose, you could abort every black baby in this country, and your crime rate would go down. That would be an impossible, ridiculous, and morally reprehensible thing to do, but your crime rate would go down. So these far-out, these far-reaching, extensive extrapolations are, I think, tricky."

In both cases, these gentlemen misunderstood the crux of people's anger: the latent belief context that generated these hypotheses. In Mr. Bennett's case, the statement is particularly egregious because the conversation and context of the discussion had nothing to do with Blacks. The conversation was about abortion, the solvency of Social Security, and crime. But as his statement showed, it is his, and others, belief that blacks are inherently criminal. And this brought to the surface his abort black babies to reduce crime "hypothesis."

Mr. Summer's situation is more subtle. Innate differences or not, women, minorities, whomever should have equal opportunity and equal access, and they do not. This is the larger issue, not innateness. As long as innateness is seen as a reason to exclude, representation by women, minorities, differing personalities, and what have you will always be scarce. And the unspoken beliefs around innate differences are potentially a root cause of the inequality, not innateness itself. Thus, women could push the argument the other way that innateness biases perpetrated by men, who cannot relate to feminine differences, is the true problem, not vice versa.

The sadder reality is reflected in the actions that underlie these "hypothetical" beliefs, not just in Dr. Summers or Mr. Bennett, but in others like them who declare, "I am not biased or racist," but *act* as if they are.

All That Said ...

You now have a fuller grasp of the multi-dimensional nature of belief. Beginning with the first dimension, we examined why we categorize. It helps us make sense of our world. Next we discussed how the stimuli we categorize stay with us once planted in our minds. We use these stimuli to unwaveringly determine the truth of an uncertainty and to assess the significance to us. These stimuli operate covertly and overtly to guide our actions and help us survive and maintain our well-being.

The various disciplines that grew from philosophy each contributed greatly to being able to complete the definition of belief. With this definition, the five characteristics of purpose can best be understood. In the chapters that follow, belief plays a leading role, among other factors, in our ability to grow, change, and evolve as we strive to make purpose work. Let's see how this happens.

CHAPTER 3

The 3,000 Year Long Search

Our Context for Belief

How would you prove to a brilliant mathematician that love exists? In the Academy Award-winning movie *A Beautiful Mind*, John Nash wants to know that the love he feels for his wife-to-be is reciprocated. A mathematical genius, he requests a proof of her love. "I need to know that love exists," said John Nash. "You mean like a proof?" she replies. "Yes." "Well, you believe in the universe correct?" "Yes, I do." "How do you know that it exists?" "Well I've reviewed the mathematical equations, and I trust their reasonableness based on that examination?" "But you don't *know* that the universe exists." "Nooo, I don't." "So you just believe." "Yes, I do." "Well, that's how love is, you don't really know, you simply believe."

For millennia, philosophers have pondered the basis under which belief can be justified as knowledge. We derive our present day understanding and context of belief from this journey in search of a kind of "truth." This truth was to help us determine, "who we are," "how we should live together," "what our purposes are," "what is real or what is not," and "what do we know and how do we come to know." While the questions are extremely insightful and valid, even today, the guidance for how we might determine the answers to these matters left us lacking. Lacking because through this guidance we inherited conceptual ideas about belief that do not provide a thoughtful, modern day context: not for everyday use and surely not for use as means to help us grow our companies and ourselves. This fact is sobering considering the importance of beliefs in personal and professional life. Through neglect, oversight, or flawed reasoning, characterization of belief has left a gap in our understanding of the productive and unproductive aspects of a vital mental construct. To understand these historical underpinnings and their present day effect, this chapter takes you on a 3,000 yearlong journey: A journey to understand our context for belief.

Clearing the Muddy Waters of Belief

Like many features of evolution, mutations and derivations do not always occur as one might have wished in hindsight. As we will explore in detail, philosophy evolved as a scientific discipline and began other disciplines that tackled with greater specificity the broad range of topics originally addressed within the discipline itself. However, emotion, which is central to belief, was questioned by most philosophers and carried little interest in mid-20th century psychology, the direct offspring of philosophy. Without the inclusion of emotion, the study of many mental phenomena was rendered emotionless, leaving their understanding and explanations incomplete. Only in the last 10-15 years has this situation changed with the study of emotions gaining a prominent position in scientific disciplines and being rightfully included in all areas related to mental phenomena. With this inclusion, we acquired the ability to fill in our knowledge gap, exploring and defining the multi-dimensional character of belief as presented in chapter 2.

Still, other problems exist and persist due to philosophy's evolution. Therefore, it is important to understand how this evolution and what it implies about what we know and don't know about the nature of belief. Understanding this historical context is also important because of philosophy's impact on every major science, particularly education, business, and psychology. In particular, we should be aware of what I have termed "epistemological overhang." This phenomenon pervades our educational and business environments and stifles our ability to productively adopt varying forms of learning and thinking styles. The epistemological overhang issues relevant to us that stem from our philosophically-defined basis of knowledge and belief include:

- Limited acceptance of varying thinking styles which inhibit the conception of self;
- Lack of motivation, notably in learning, due to the inhibition of thinking styles;
- Exaggerated or demoralized expectations of the future based on exposure to sensory data;
- Biased judgments regarding knowledge and intelligence due to temperament and reflected in differing thinking styles; and
- Perpetuated knowledge and inclusion biases that limit insight, innovation, evolution, change, and growth of individuals, societies, and its organizations.

Elements of these theories and its effects are deeply rooted in our societal structures. In chapters 4 through 8, we will discuss the implications and effects of these structural impediments to people's full use of knowledge and belief in their organizational and personal environments.

Also, to the extent that we have prejudicial views of the nature of belief, we can trace where those views might stem from. We begin with natural philosophy.

The Birth of Philosophy

Now if you are reading this and wondering, "what is philosophy?" you are not alone. Philosophy, like belief, purpose, vision, values, mission, and many other affective terms we will be using and discussing throughout this book, has no clear definition. We can trace its origin pretty easily. The word is derived from the Greek term *Philosophia*, by way of Latin, and means "love of wisdom." However, any simplicity ends there. It would be easier for you, the reader, if we could provide a simple definition. Unfortunately, one simple definition doesn't work. We need two definitions.

Over the next several pages, philosophy is presented as an examination of the grounds for fundamental belief and an analysis of the basic concepts employed in the expression of such belief. Later in chapter 8, when we discuss fear, this perspective is broadened to consider philosophy as a set of basic values and attitudes toward life, nature, and society.

Current everyday use of the term philosophy generally centers on the latter definition. In the context of personal and corporate life, this is the relevant definition. But to enable us to understand the nature of belief, the historical context for how we have come to use it and perceive it in creating a philosophy of anything is salient. To make clear the intertwined link between our conceptual context of belief and how we use belief to create a philosophic stance for business, we must begin with the former definition.

The earliest philosophers, as did the future Mrs. Nash, looked to the heavens for evidence of what we can know and what we don't know. After all, gazing up into the heavens one cannot help but wonder "who we are," "why we are here," and "how this has come to be." These are natural curiosities. So, man, who, like other animals, was born with an inclination to explore and seek understanding of his environment, did what is natural. He sought answers to these amazing and perplexing questions. This questioning was the beginning of natural philosophy.

It seems natural that the first notions of science centered on questions of the universe. And, we must understand that philosophy is a science. It is a science that seeks explanation for occurrences in the material world. Such explanation cannot be derived simply through observation, although that is one facet of science. The early Chinese and Mesopotamian (now Iraq and parts of Syria) cultures provide excellent examples of exact observation and description of nature. They used these descriptions and observations to create very ordered and orderly civilizations. Many of their cultural traditions revolved around description and observation of the heavens, but understanding this phenomenon was

deemed achievable only by the Gods.

For the Chinese, the universe was explained through balancing the forces of opposites, yin and yang, and harmonizing the five elements: water, wood, metal, fire, and earth. In Mesopotamia, numerous gods maintained harmony. While Egyptians focused their energies on attainment of the afterlife, they, too, believed harmony was created by obedience to numerous gods who worked to fight *"chaos"* (i.e., uncertainty). Thus in all cases of early civilization of which we have recorded knowledge, understanding or "knowledge" of the forces of nature existed only through religion or magic. If the gods did not will it so, it was not so; or at least, that is what people believed.

We will never know why Hellenic citizens became unhappy with this state of affairs. Nonetheless, it is clear that religion was the most distinct difference between ancient civilizations. As a result, lack of religious sophistication most likely prompted Greek philosophers to seek explanations that provided reasoned and insightful knowledge of the universe's operation and man's purpose in it. Attacking these matters during four distinct periods of Greek Philosophy, Pre-Socratic philosophy, Socratic Philosophy, Hellenistic Philosophy, and the Roman Empire, they created principles that rippled through philosophic reflection into the 15th century. Against this backdrop, we need to consider evolutionary changes in philosophy, from the time of the ancient philosophers to the present day, that forever shaped philosophic inquiry and our subsequent context for belief. To start, we summarize the relevant implications below. You can keep these

issues in mind as we cover, throughout the remainder
of this chapter, pivotal transition points in the history
of philosophical thought that effect our attitudes
about belief.

1. Natural philosophers wanted to understand what was
   happening around them without needing to turn to
   ancient myths. They wanted to understand actual
   processes by studying nature itself. This resulted
   in philosophy questioning mythical or religious
   belief. And, set the stage for scientific reasoning and
   questioning speculative theorizing.

2. The ancient philosophers began with very valid
   questions about man and belief. Unfortunately, the
   meaning of questions central to their exploration, "what
   should I believe and why," were lost and distorted over
   time as modern philosophers (during the Renaissance)
   began to expound the theory of knowledge.

3. Thus, philosophy lost sight of the very issue it
   sought to address: Belief. With the exception of the
   Enlightenment philosopher David Hume, who made
   belief central to his treatise, thoughtful consideration
   of "what is belief?" has been a philosophical oversight.
   The consequence is that up to the end of the 20th
   century we made little progress in understanding
   belief, at the individual or societal level.

4. Historical overhang from the theory of knowledge
   debate, which began during the Renaissance,
   compounded the problem of understanding belief.
   Along with prejudicial views of knowledge, this long-
   standing debate created structural impediments to
   full consideration of knowledge by limiting relevance
   of various forms of intelligence.

5. The context for belief was further neglected when
   philosophy segmented into other areas of science,

notably psychology. Emotion, which is central to belief, was given sparse (and sometimes harsh) treatment under this division, leaving us with an emotion-laden, ambiguous view of belief, until recent times.

To obtain a better appreciation for how these historical by-products came about, we need to consider why the natural philosophers came to question the basis of belief.

Questioning of the Basis of Belief

Natural philosophy surfaced during the pre-Socratic epoch. It was termed "natural philosophy" because inquiries speculated on the basic underlying substance of nature. We only know of these musings through later philosophers such as Aristotle and Plato, who provided only the conclusions reached without sharing insight into how they were derived. This context leads to the assumption that natural philosophers launched into an attack on the origin of the universe ignoring or avoiding the issue of the possibilities and extent of human knowledge. This question becomes central to one area of philosophy after the Middle Ages. Another notable characteristic of natural philosophy is the complete fusion of philosophy and science. Astronomy, mathematics, anthropology, and the beginnings of medicine were all included within the scope of philosophy. Although medicine was the first to break away into a separate discipline, other disciplines remained under the heading of philosophy until the end of the Hellenistic Age (c. 330 AD), more than eight centuries later.

While lack of religious sophistication was the

primary reason for the Greeks seeking an answer to " who are we" through natural philosophy, there were also other tangential issues. Having expanded westward in the 8th century BC to lands such as southern Italy, Sicily, and Turkey, political and tribal strife led to rule by tyrants. Over time, the Hellenic people came to feel oppressed within the environment, and old traditions and establishments, even for the aristocracy, which the natural philosophers represented, no longer held within the community. This gradual disenfranchisement and instability lead naturally to questions of "who one is' within an unfamiliar and changing environment. Historical record of internment often provides example of people's search for meaning when conditions severely threaten the normalcy of existence. Given these circumstances, the Greeks had two choices: find solace in the changing religious landscape or look within the individual for answers. Obviously, the natural philosophers chose to look inside themselves.

The answers arrived at significantly contributed to the development of scientific reasoning. In mathematics, the work of the Pythagorean School is best known for the development of the *Pythagorean Theorem*. However, in music, they laid the foundation for musical therapy and discovered that musical intervals are expressed as numerical proportions as well as the more specific idea of harmonic "means." The science of logic can be traced to the Eleatic School, while the Heraclitean School presaged the theory of energy. Most impressive, however, is the work of the Atomists School. Through the scientific and philosophic work of Democritus, the theory of the atom was born, along with a detailed treatise of the determination of nature on the basis of physical laws.

Understandings of the material world accomplished by the natural philosophers derived from a fusion of philosophy and science. This fusion was borne out of necessity. Lacking formal divisions, they explored areas of science, as they deemed relevant. No artificial boundaries of scientific domain or subject matter experts existed to dictate where they should and should not explore. Further, the absence of "subject matter expertise" gave them the freedom to judge their work based on their own tests for reasonableness and satisfactory treatment. Checks and balances were created through students and other philosophic schools having the freedom to question and evolve their own thinking, which naturally occurred. This peer-critique process fueled theory evolution through review and rebuttal. Hence, fusion of science and philosophy enabled understanding and provided a necessary reference pool of sensory data sources for speculative inquiry to consider the material world and its counteracting properties from various scientific domains.

Reviewing the finding of these first scientific thinkers and philosophers, one is struck by the depth of their insight. This feat is considerably remarkable when juxtaposed against the tools at their disposal. These included sensory observation, reason, intuition, self-derived scientific principles, and a willingness to speculate. Because these pioneers sought to explain the world, the world gained a better perspective on how to assess its own environment without recourse to mysticism or religion. One was free to believe as an individual about "who he was." The primacy of this fact still serves the free world. But, this freedom is not without limits. As we discuss shortly, the Sophists challenged the validity of speculative inquiry and began to set the ground rules for how belief might be justified as knowledge.

From this time, the foundation was laid for the Rationalist and Empiricist theories of knowledge (as they would later be called) that followed. The nature and implications of these theories will be examined when we consider the manner in which philosophers went about "Defining the Basis of Knowledge."

The first philosophers dug the substructure, enabling the individual to exert his own intelligence to ask "who he was." They also laid within that substructure the foundation upon which could be built a solid structure of knowledge using either reason, sensation, intuition, or some combination as a method to guide the discovery process. But Hellenic society continued to change, and, particularly for ancient Athens, old tyrannical rulers gave way to fledgling democracies. Alas, once again, philosophers reassessed meaning within their world.

Democracy's birth in ancient Athens created a need for education amongst the citizenry to facilitate self-government. This need was filled by the evolution of a category of philosophers called 'Sophists.' Moving away from speculative inquiry, Sophists focused their concerns on the individual and the practicalities of his role in society. This shift changed the focus of belief from singularly religious (the nature of existence) to include secular issues, where it remains to this day. For the Sophist, man had no hope of understanding "who he was" in the cosmos. A leading Sophist, Gorgias, argued, "nothing really exists, that if anything did exist it could not be known, and that if knowledge were possible, it could not be communicated." Such an assessment was decided considering the ability of man to know with certainty, thus laying the seed of skepticism. Given their skepticism, the Sophists shifted philosophical questioning more practically to man's role in society: "why are we here" and "how do we live together." These questions were, of course, not unhelpful as Greek-style government, culture, and other societal concepts laid the foundations for evolution of Western civilization. While history is not really kind to the Sophists, their work benefited Greek society by creating formal educational structures.

In their quest for practicality, Sophists did not attempt to determine the first causes of things. They focused on experience and sought to amass the greatest amount of information from all aspects of life. They drew only particular conclusions (partially of a theoretical nature): the possibility or impossibility of knowledge; the beginning and progress of human civilization; the origin and structure of language. Most elements focused on practical issues such as the appropriate and efficient arrangement of the individual's life and society. In this manner, their method was empiric-inductive. And, this experienced-based, determinative approach commenced with a part of the theory of knowledge, which was later to become empiricism.

Although, Plato disliked the Sophists and his influence contributed to their eventual demise, in establishing the Academy, he extended their flame of formal education amongst Athenian citizenry. He also sought to address their skepticism in his Theory of Ideas. Socrates, of course, principally influenced Plato. It was Socrates' strong belief that he must help man learn to think for himself and determine what is principled and ethical according to universal norms through reason. Plato made it his life's work to fulfill this dream of Socrates. In this regard, it is then in the work of Plato that we find the strongest support for a purely rational approach to knowledge. This is climatically argued in his Theory of Ideas.

His arguments are later re-considered by his star pupil, Aristotle. Aristotle tutored Alexander the Great and founded the Lyceum, in 335 BC, in a grove sacred to Apollo Lyceius, and sent philosophy on its course with a strong sail of philosophical principles that would carry the day well into the 17[h] century. It was determined through the independent dialectics of Aristotle that the root of knowledge is generalized through experience (i.e., sensation); however, he maintained that abstract knowledge, gained through reasoning, was man's distinguishing characteristic. Since reason is completely empty until we have sensed something, it is by reasoning what we sense that we develop concepts ("Ideas" as Plato defined them).

As we move to the next section to discuss the basis of knowledge, it is important to keep these last thoughts of Aristotle's in mind. Interestingly, later philosophers did not necessarily see human understanding as being a balance of two mental faculties: some saw it as a dominance of one faculty to the exclusion of the other. Could you image life relying only on reasoning or only on your sensory experience? Delving into "Defining the Basis of Knowledge," you will glimpse how and why you perceive the world contextually when relying predominantly on one mental faculty.

Defining the Basis of Knowledge

The Theory of Knowledge, as it is sometimes referred to, is expounded under the branch of philosophy termed "Epistemology." The word epistemology derives from the Greek terms *episteme,* meaning "knowledge," and *logos,* meaning "reason." There are two key questions to epistemological pursuits: "What do we know?" and "How do we know?" From these two questions, many issues cascade downward, such as the definition of knowledge, the degree of certainty of knowledge, the relation between the knower and the known, and others. All of which combine to illustrate the complexity of knowing. Yet, most of us think we know a lot; unlike Socrates, who thought he knew nothing. Epistemologists share Socrates view of what we know. From the time of the pre-Socratic philosophers forward, observations of the material world have continuously presented puzzles and challenges to our ability to understand the nature, scope, and limitations of knowledge. These puzzles and challenges led philosophers to assert that most of what man accepts as knowledge is dubious at best and chimerical at worst. But, they refused to accept that man was doomed to existence without meaningful knowledge. Rejecting such a fate, every great philosopher has contributed literature supporting a theory of knowledge. Though the puzzles and anomalies considered by these thinkers cover a vast terrain of ideas and observations, a central theme underlies many of their analyses of knowledge and their resulting treatises to understanding knowledge. This theme is the issue of sense experience versus reason, and it forms part of the basis of knowledge.

These views represent two dimensions to the temperament of all humans as opposed to a necessary truth in respect to *the* source of knowledge. We all have an element of pre-wiring that conditions us to prefer some things to other things, and philosophers (although extraordinary thinkers) are no different in this regard than the rest of us. Their respective thinking style biases colored their views of what was the "true" source of knowledge. Later generations, knowing and unknowingly, adopted and inherited these views contributing to what we earlier termed "epistemological overhang." It exists due to institutions' promotion of one type of knowledge or thinking style over another. For example, some publishing houses have a strong bias for empirical studies. American business has a strong bias towards "pragmatic" views, which stems from Pragmatism, which is a derivative school of thought with empiricist tendencies. In academic disciplines, physics, led by Einstein's *Theory of Relativity*, is biased towards a mathematical (rational) explanation of universal forces, while biology, which is steeped in cause and effect study, is clearly empirically driven. This is a small sample; however, in reality, epistemological overhang impacts almost all institutional domains of society.

It is not clear that pre-20th century philosophers themselves would have created such stark distinctions. However, no discipline gets to write its own history. At some point, philosophy historians drew a line in the sand. Philosophers became either supporters of sense experience, known as Empiricists, or supporters of reason, known as Rationalists, with a few notable exceptions (particularly, the Idealists and Pragmatists). As the influence of these divergent philosophical systems permeated society, these categories came to impact how we defined, assessed, and acquired knowledge. Epistemological overhang persists because we suffer an unwillingness to expand our belief systems to accept a source of knowledge as relevant or choose to believe one to be superior to the other. Understanding the existence of these beliefs due to epistemological overhang and our own temperamental biases is the first step in appreciating the many sources of mental processing knowledge and expanding our perception of relevant beliefs. Returning to the pre-Socratic philosophers, we will briefly trace how these historical categories came about and discuss how epistemological overhang impacts us today.

The Rise of Epistemology

It was actually during the epoch of natural philosophy that the basis of knowledge ("justifiable belief" as defined by Plato) was introduced. Casting the first stone was Heraclitus (c. 544-484) who was born in Ephesus, the most important Greek city in Ionian Asia Minor, which contained the Temple of Artemis, one of the Seven Wonders of the ancient world. Heraclitus, born an aristocrat, held contempt for the activities and opinions of men. His disdain was so great that he removed himself from public life and sought solace and reflection at the Temple of

Artemis. In his philosophical work, Heraclitus, like other philosophers of his time, worked to discover the basic substance underlying all material things. Given his opinion of man, Heraclitus was consciously aware of the limitation of human knowledge, and he recognized the relativity of human ideas. Rather than such limitations impacting his attempt to discover "who are we," it came to color his view on how man came to know. In the opinion of Heraclitus, everything "flowed" and nothing is permanent. There was an unceasing changing of things, and the world was always subject to new modifications. The complete immutability of being (because everything returns back to its original form "fire"), precipitated his rejection of the world of the senses as they give the illusion of a permanent being, but he recognized the ever-changing substance of fire as the reality behind it.

The antithesis to Heraclitus is reasoned in the Philosophy of Parmenides of Elea (c.540-470). Parmenides was also an aristocrat, as were all the natural philosophers. Though he was an excellent political statesman, Ameinias of the Pythagorean School convinced him to give up his political career for a life of philosophic pursuit. The philosophy of Parmenides was extreme, which is possibly why it evoked strong reactions from the philosophers to follow him. Still, posterity is indebted to him for his metaphysical opposition of being and thought, which set the stage for the Atomist's theory and Plato's Theory of Ideas.

Parmenides rejected Heraclitus' proposition of a permanent being and the notion that everything flows. For Parmenides, the world was unchangeable, "Nothing can come out of nothing." And, nothing that exists can become nothing. While realizing that nature is in a constant state of change of becoming and passing away, like Heraclitus, he believed this to be a perceptual illusion, blatantly rejecting sensual experience. Further, because he could find no reason to accept Heraclitus' assertion that a permanent being, fire, changes into other forms, he regarded it as impossible. In opposition to this view and in denial of sensual experience, Parmenides "logically" asserted that being was unchangeable. As an illustration, Parmenides' philosophy demonstrates a somewhat extreme, but relevant, Rationalist theory of knowledge.

The issue of permanence provided a challenge that became the starting point for Plato's Theory of Ideas. Plato accepted that genuine knowledge must be permanent and durable. In his view, this represented the world of thought. Plato surmised that what we apprehend with our senses are particulars—Hackneys, Shetlands, Africans, Europeans—that are not necessarily lasting (e.g., many species of the animal kingdom as well as languages are now extinct). Common and enduring qualities that define a thing—the *Equidae* (horse) or *Homo sapiens* (human) species from the animal kingdom—Plato defined as an *idea*: "We suppose an idea to exist when we give the same name to many things." Today, we call this category of similar things a *concept*, as Aristotle later defined it, or a form.

Ideas, and their immutability, drive Plato's assertion that reason is the source of knowledge.

Only through reason can mankind apprehend the common and enduring qualities of a thing through the dialectic method. The dialectic (as we will recall from freshman year philosophy) is an exploration based on question and answer. This exploration is conducted in order to grasp conceptually that which is. For Plato, this becomes a theory of science, of knowing the true reality of things. It is also therefore a search for the defining nature of things and, as a result, a search for knowledge.

While Plato's philosophy will forever stand as the voice of rational thinking, René Descartes (1596-1650) is considered the founder of modern Rationalism. Of course, Descartes led us to believe that "I think; therefore, I am." His philosophy combined the influences of the past into an original synthesis that seemed sympathetic to the scientific temper of the age. In spite of appearances, his tombstone reads: "He who hid well, lived well." This suggests he may not have been as sympathetic as he appeared. Still, in the minds of historians, he is the originator of the modern spirit of philosophy. A great mathematician, he invented analytic geometry and made many physical and anatomical experiments. In his *Principia,* Descartes defined philosophy as "the study of wisdom" or "the perfect knowledge of all one can know." Its chief utility is "for the conduct of life" (morals), "the conservation of health" (medicine), and "the invention of all the arts" (mechanics).

Descartes wrote his philosophy as a challenge to Skepticism, the doctrine that man cannot know the truth about the riddles of nature and of the universe. He challenged the skeptics by asserting certain knowledge of his own existence. This certain knowledge, he proved using his reasoning abilities and the mental processing faculties of intuition and deduction. But, if man could only know that he existed, life would be narrow and depressing. Descartes refused to accept such a state of affairs and sought other things that could be grasped with intuitive certainty. From this premise, Descartes formed a view of God as a perfect entity suggesting we can have an idea of perfect entity. As we are imperfect, the idea of a perfect entity represents an innate idea not derivable from experience. Thus, in agreement with Socrates and Plato, Descartes perceived the source of knowledge to be man's ability to reason: to go beyond his outer reality to define the nature of a thing. He saw the basic, certain, and defining quality of man as the ability to think and of God as being a perfect entity. As he considered these as abstractions not perceived or acquired through sense experience, the basis of knowledge must then derive innately from man's ability to reason.

It is clear, in these abbreviated versions of the epistemologies of Plato and Descartes, that through abstractions and mathematical concepts, Rationalists (Latin *ratio*, meaning "reason") have attempted to articulate the role of reason in allowing human beings to understand the world they live in. For Rationalists, this is the true source of knowledge. Rationalists believe this because mathematics and abstractions represent a class of truths that the intellect can grasp directly. Archimedes' Principle is a simple illustration of this. During the normal course of taking a bath, one automatically considers the height of the water level in the bath. Why? When your body is submersed in the water, its volume will displace the water from its original level. This displacement represents the weight of your body. Now, you may or may not know the mathematical equation that these counteracting forces correspond to, but you can grasp the principle directly. This is the point Rationalists sought to get across. Like Michael Faraday, who was terrible at mathematics, but great at physics, which supposedly depends on mathematics, we can all grasp the principles of a thing without necessarily being able to explain in theoretical terms why that thing works in a particular manner. In demonstrating the *a priori* (pre-existing) nature of knowledge through examples, the Rationalists insist they have demonstrated that such knowledge is innate, not learned from experience. While Rationalists hold reason as a superior form of knowledge, most, unlike Parmenides, do not deny that sensory perception plays a role in knowledge. They believe it plays an important role in criticizing and shaping reason. In this vein, the senses provide a test of the principles that form rational arguments. Sense experience does this because it enables one to establish regular association of phenomena, like the triangularity of triangles. Nevertheless, sense experience cannot explain *why* it should happen or determine that it had to happen (i.e., predict the occurrence). For these reasons, Rationalists give sense experience a minor and supporting role in their theories of knowledge.

That gives us one side of the coin, the rationalist view. Now, let us consider the world dominated by sense experience. We mentioned that the earliest

Empiricists were the Sophists, and that Gorgias was a leader among them. Actually, we still use sayings from the Sophists, such as "Man is the measure of all things." This famous maxim is attributed to Protagoras and is typical of the Sophists' attitude. Protagoras claimed that individuals have the right to judge matters for themselves and denied that we have objective knowledge. He believed that truth was subjective because different things hold true for different people. Moreover, he believed that we cannot prove one person's belief to be objectively correct and another's incorrect. The Stoics and the Epicureans joined the Sophists in their empirical stance (although not in this particular assertion). Despite their early empiric notions, when we speak of empiricists, generally we are referring to the British Empiricists: John Locke, George Berkeley, and David Hume.

The British Empiricists took the stance that beliefs are to be accepted and acted upon only if they first have been confirmed by actual experience. In this way, empiricism is always critical, resistant to the pretensions of speculative philosophy, as we saw first with the Sophists, and we will soon see in the philosophies of Locke and Hume. In its extreme form, empiricism leads to the conclusion that not only does all knowledge start from experience, but also that it can never get beyond experience. This stance is voiced loudly in the doctrine of Hume.

Latin derived its *empiricus* from the Greek: *peira*, meaning "trial" or "experiment," *empiros*, meaning "skilled," and *empeiria*, meaning "experience." The earliest use refers to a school of physicians, *empiricus*, as opposed to a methodology. The empiricus based their practice on experience and not on theories drawn from general philosophies. Sir Francis Bacon first used the category "empiricist." However, he was referring to scientists, not philosophers. Later, in the nineteenth century, historians seized the opportunity to create a great debate amongst opposing philosophical schools of thought. In this debate, Thomas Kant, a German philosopher, was credited as the "genius" that synthesized their opposing doctrines. This historical interpretation created the birth of the Rationalist and the Empiricist.

We mentioned earlier, the historical significance of Aristotle's philosophy, which reigned until the end of the middle ages. In the early phases of Renaissance philosophy, Aristotelian logic was attacked, and the role of observation was brought to the forefront. Sir Francis Bacon (1561–1626) was the outstanding apostle of Renaissance Empiricism, who led the charge for observation in scientific discovery.   Sir Francis was the advocate of a vast new program for the advancement of learning and reformation of the scientific method.   He conceived of philosophy as a method that should re-establish natural science upon a firm foundation. With a profound belief in the superiority of observation, he created laws and generalizations, such as his conception of forms. This doctrine was quite un-Platonic, as a form represented a permanent geometric or mechanical structure, not an abstract essence as Plato had viewed it. However of importance to us is his single-minded advocacy of experience as the only source of valid knowledge and his profound enthusiasm for the perfection of natural science. This empiricism inspired the English philosophers of science during the 19th century.

Though Bacon was an apostle for empiricism, John Locke (1632-1704) provided the first elaborate and influential philosophical system of Empiricism. Like Aristotle, a millennium earlier, Locke's philosophy significantly influenced the larger society, particularly educational institutions. For education, Locke is noteworthy, both for his general theory of knowledge and for his ideas on the education of youth. Locke thought of the mind as a "blank tablet" prior to experience, a position that some still hold, but he did not claim that all minds are equal. He insisted, in *Some Thoughts Concerning Education*, that some minds have a greater intellectual potential than others. Locke's empiricism expressed his belief that ideas originate in experience. In *An Essay Concerning Human Understanding*, he argued that ideas come from two "fountains" of experience: *sensation*, through which the senses convey perceptions into the mind, and *reflection*, whereby the mind works with the perceptions, forming ideas. For Locke, believing, along with perceiving, thinking, doubting, reasoning, and knowing, is an example of a reflection.

Empiricists believe there is nothing in the mind until the senses place it there. Recall that it was actually Aristotle, who first said this, although he is considered a Rationalist. Locke took this further by suggesting that all of the concepts in our minds are built up from simple sense experiences. Locke compared the mind to an unfurnished room. Ultimately, we begin to place things in the room, and then, we begin to sense the world around us through sights, smells, tastes, feelings, and sounds. Through these experiences we begin to capture what Locke called *simple ideas of sense*. The mind does not accept these perceptions passively; it actively engages with them. Like furniture in a room, it sorts them into categories through *reflection*. This is why he distinguishes between sensation and reflection. In categorizing sensations into reflections, complex ideas are formed in the mind. A simple example illustrating this notion is the complex idea of an apple. When one first eats an apple, one experiences its color, shape, smell, flavor, and hears a sound when it's bitten. After many similar experiences, one forms the *complex idea* of an apple based on these prior simple sensual experiences. Having had this sensual experience one has certain knowledge of an apple, which is a complex idea.

David Hume (1711-1776), the Scottish philosopher, said that he conceived the idea of his philosophy when he was 15 years old. His most important work, *A Treatise of Human Nature*, was published when he was 28 years old. Hume had hopes of greatness and wished to become the Sir Isaac Newton of philosophy by formulating universal principles to explain "all effects from the simplest and fewest causes," but a boundary condition on these principles is that they "cannot go beyond experience." A bit of a dramatic, Hume believed we must clean up our thoughts, ideas, and book collections from prior philosophical periods that contained ambiguous concepts and thought constructions. "If we take in our hands any volume... let us ask: 'Does it contain any abstract reasoning concerning quantity or number? Does it contain any experimental reasoning concerning matter of fact and existence? Commit it then to the flames, for it can contain nothing but sophistry and illusion." Like Parmenides, Hume's philosophy was extreme, but his skepticism about philosophical empiricism raised questions about the possibility of knowledge that contemporary philosophers still struggle to resolve. He questioned the relationship of cause and effect where we rely on past experience to predict the future, stating that it was not rational. Hume carried these notions so far as to question the existence of the mind, emphasizing that the mind, body, and casual connection can be taken only as far as one's experience with them. For Hume, man can never get beyond his own experience. Though extreme, Hume's observations of perception and causation provide a very relevant context for belief.

Hume conceived of our ability to know as deriving from two kinds of perceptions: impressions and ideas. Impressions are the immediate sensation of external reality and ideas represent the memory of impressions. An example would be hitting your knee on a coffee table. The impression is the sensation (feeling experience) of pain caused by the knee interacting forcefully with a hard object, the table. On seeing the resultant bruise, afterward you reflect on hurting yourself and may recall the pain you felt. Thus, ideas are faint images of the lively impressions that we experience in the real world. These experiences are the direct cause of the ideas that are formed in the mind through reflection. Hume concluded that ideas and impressions can be either simple or complex. Going back to the Lockean example, the experience of eating an apple would represent a complex impression. Recall that in the Humean world, we cannot get beyond experience, so the mind must construct complex ideas from simple impressions. Consider the complex idea of "pearly gates." Man has had the experience of seeing pearls and the experience of seeing gates. To create the idea of "pearl gates," the mind of man imaginatively connects the two forming a complex idea that does not exist in the physical world. If it could not be traced to sense perceptions, Hume declared we should "dismiss all this meaningless nonsense which long has dominated metaphysical thought and brought it into disrepute."

But, he wasn't finished. Hume also questioned reasoning as the source of causal understanding. To go straight to the point, Hume surmised that we predict causal relations out of custom, not through reasoning. If we see one billiard ball strike another billiard ball and observe the effect of one rolling due to the impact of the other, we expect a similar occurrence in the future. Similarly, we monitor the height of the bathwater because we know the water level will change when we get into the tub. Why? We have become accustomed to this happening from previous experience. The idea of habit shaping perception is not lost on creativity consultants. "Thinking like a child" goes straight to the heart of Hume's philosophy of experience. We expect occurrences to happen because we have become accustomed to them happening: stones falling to the ground, trees shedding leaves, etc. Hume's issue with the law of causation is important for our understanding of belief. By challenging the idea that we can know based on cause and effect when we have not actually *experienced* the cause, he appropriately pointed out that *expectation* is driving perceived knowledge. Expectation is not a genuine expression of cause and effect and, thus, does not represent a prediction in the scientific sense. So, Hume's observation raises an interesting question. Does our everyday observation of an occurrence that we come to treat as an expectation count as knowledge? We will present an answer in the next chapter and discuss the issue of belief as expectations in Chapter 6.

Earlier, we questioned the appropriateness of philosophers standing on one side of the knowledge formation argument versus another. While we can see in hindsight the contextual issues resulting from this, we must not lose sight of what was gained from the debate. In choosing a side (despite mental-processing biases), philosophers gave us much food-for-thought on the complexity of human mental faculties, which underlie the construction of our beliefs. We would be the better for this had we also not let human temperament cloud our ability to draw objective insight from what philosophy was struggling to teach us. In this vain, Immanuel Kant, a German philosopher who responded to Hume's philosophy, and William James, a American philosopher who is considered one of the founders of Pragmatism, both attempted to illustrate the objective benefits of these arguments.

We now continue our journey towards understanding the context for modern day belief. In this next stop on our uncertain destination, we examine the road traveled from natural philosophy to cognitive psychology, where today's context for belief resides.

Spawning Various Paths to Knowledge

The birth of science and the birth of philosophy are co-joined through the birth of natural philosophy. In this respect, science and philosophy in the Western Hemisphere emanate from natural philosophy. As we have already mentioned, many organizational environments have, during some period of their existence been influenced by a philosophical heritage. We continue our journey to understand our modern day context of belief by tracing the evolution of natural philosophy into the domain of cognitive psychology. During this part of our travels, we will seek out the roots to the theories of knowledge that have shaped our belief context through the tutelage of the social sciences.

It should be pointed out that the path that we are about to follow is related principally to the Western Hemisphere (Egypt and Mesopotamia will be touched on). Ancient Chinese science was far more advanced than the West up until the Renaissance. It was very advanced in chemistry (i.e., alchemy), medicine, geology, geography, and technology. We don't know a lot about ancient Indian science, because scholars haven't really studied it that closely. We do know that ancient Indian mathematics was quite advanced, particularly in geometry and algebra. The Mayans in Central America (although this is in the Western Hemisphere) we know about, but they will not be discussed. With that backdrop, let's continue on our journey.

Science and philosophy have much in common. Both seek to help man sort out and bring order to that which hinders clarity in our daily lives. Both quests for knowledge started many millennia ago and each has had periods of great productivity and periods of decline. Both have, at periods in time, been questioned for their usefulness to society and their impact on society. Both have taken us on a journey with an uncertain destination.

Evidence of science can be traced archaeologically to most civilizations that we know of in the ancient world. Prehistoric humans were close observers of nature. Archaeological features, particularly sundials, make this fact obvious. The oldest time device, the gnomon, dates back to 3500 BC. Egypt has the best-preserved sundial that dates back to the 8th century BC. Understanding the time of day and the seasons was crucial for prehistoric man's ability to comprehend the migration habits of animals, which they depended on for survival. Once agriculture was invented, the time to plant and harvest could only be predicted by following the changing rhythms of the universe from season to season. As well, early sea wanderers relied heavily on astronomical observation to guide them home safely from their travels. These fundamental needs for basic survival made science, then simply the observation and recording of nature, crucial to the existence of man.

Historians believe that the growth of astronomy fueled the growth of mathematics. In ancient Mesopotamia, mathematics and astronomy thrived. Mesopotamians knew the Pythagorean relationship well and used it frequently. Having created degrees, minutes, and seconds, they also developed a numbering system based on 60 that was adapted to arithmetic. Such advances contributed to sophistication in mathematics that went far beyond the requirements of daily life. In astronomy, they were unrivaled in the ancient world.

As in philosophy, ancient Greek science had a significant influence on the development of modern science in the West. Hellenic science was built on the natural philosophers Thales of Miletus (c. 624-546 BC) and Pythagoras. Earlier, you were introduced to Pythagoras. Thales was renowned as one of the legendary Seven Wise Men, or *Sophoi*, of antiquity. *Sophoi* means inventiveness and practical wisdom. Thales, considered the first Greek philosopher, constructed the first purely natural explanation of the origin of the world free of mythological construction. He hypothesized that everything came from water—based on the discovery of fossil sea animals. It was the critic of Thales' explanation that instigated the later intellectual explosion that became ancient Greek Philosophy. Recall that natural philosopher's theories were open to critique. Well, it was one of Thales' pupils, Anaximander, who argued that water could not be the basic substance of the universe. He asserted logically that water, which was wet, has an opposite, which is dry. If everything comes from water, that precludes all of the dry things in the world. Thales was, of course, wrong. However, this process of stating a hypothesis and allowing scrutiny of it through reasoning, created the birth of a critical tradition that was fundamental to the advancement of science. This advancement moved natural scientists away from simple observation and recording towards critical analysis. Later testing, experimentation, and verification would follow. These steps form the basis of today's scientific method.

Hellenic science reached its zenith, though, with Aristotle and Archimedes. Many of us know of Archimedes (c, 290–212 BC) for one reason or another. We will glance at his many accomplishments in a moment. Snippets of Aristotle's philosophy have already been touched on; now, we will consider his scientific accomplishments. Aristotle demonstrated great skill in understanding observations in nature. He accomplished this by assessing the purpose of a thing, its form, and the origin of its form. As an example of the importance of his insight, in biology, his observations of marine life were unrivaled for 22 centuries. In general, his biological framework was used as a template until the work of Charles Darwin in the 1850s.

Archimedes was equally prolific. Although he probably didn't say, "Give me a place to stand, and I'll move the world," we associate him with it. Archimedes resided for most of his life in Syracuse, a Greek city-state in Sicily. Having developed Archimedes' Principle discussed earlier, he is the founder of hydrostatics. Archimedes determined the proportion of gold and silver in Heiron's wreath by weighing it in water. All we non-scientists care about, however, is that he supposedly leaped from his bath, where he got the idea, and ran naked through the streets shouting "Eureka!" Oh, and the lever: he demonstrated the law of the lever, too.

To understand the world, philosophy dwelled deeply within many domains of science. But as we mentioned earlier, however, not all scientists felt the need to remain closely tied to the apron strings of mother philosophy. The first discipline to seek maturity in its own right was medicine. Greek physicians made a great deal of progress in understanding the human body. Many of us know Hippocrates (of the Hippocratic Oath). He is considered the father of medicine. Hippocrates (c. 460-377 BC) observed the effect of food, occupation, and climate in causing disease. Through these studies, published in the treatise *De Natura Homini* ("On the Nature of Man"), he emphasized that disease is a natural, not spiritual, phenomenon and the body's natural ability to heal itself. If Hippocrates is considered the father of medicine, Galen of Pergamum is surely the first son. Galen (c. 129-216 AD), a physician, writer, and philosopher, exerted significant influence on medical theory and practice in Europe from the Middle Ages until the mid-17th century. We discuss an aspect of Galen's work "temperament," in Chapter 4. Other physiological elements of Galen's work are of more importance to us here because modern day psychology stems both from physiology and philosophy. Thus, Galen—philosopher and physiologist—began a dual path toward the study of the mind. Ironically, it was also the overthrow of Galenian theories by English physician Harvey Williams, through his publication on the circulation of blood in 1628, which signaled the emergence of modern science.

During the mid-1800s, physiologists began studying the human brain and nervous system, paying particular attention to sensation. In the 1850s, Herman von Helmholtz located the sensory receptors in the ear and eye, and Gustav Fechner founded *psychophysics,* the study of the relationship between physical stimuli and related sensations created by that stimuli. Paul Broca located the area of the left hemisphere of our brain that enables fluent speech, while Carl Wernicke located the area that allows us to comprehend speech. They each have an area of the brain named after them. All the while, modern philosophy, having made the shift from the ancient world and the Middle Ages, continued to explore numerous topics of mind, through epistemology as well as through metaphysics.

Psychology did not find the strength or desire to cut the apron strings from philosophy until 1879, many millennia later. Five years earlier in North America, Harvard University Professor William James offered the first course in Psychology. William James is best known for his classic *Will to Believe*. On psychology, James published a two volume book entitled *Principles of Psychology* in 1890. Over time, it became the leading psychology textbook in America. But, it was at the University of Leipzig, in Germany, that physiologist Wilhelm Wundt established the first laboratory dedicated to the scientific study of the mind. This event signaled the birth of psychology as a formal science. Wundt's approaches centered on systematic and rigorous observation of individuals, and the primary research method was introspection. From these meager starting points, psychology began to flourish quickly in US and in Europe, although the paths to understanding the mind were divided quite nationalistically.

Cognitive psychology transitioned to a league of its own following three distinct waves of psychological theorizing: Psychoanalysis, Behaviorism, and Humanism. However for the first twenty years preceding the rise of these disciplines, two schools of thought dominated the field: Functionalism and Structuralism. Functionalism promoted understanding the function of consciousness. William James advocated this field of study, having been influenced by the work of Charles Darwin. Darwin's work demonstrated that all species adapt to a particular function for the purpose of survival. James felt that man's consciousness should be understood on those terms. William Wundt promoted the competing school of thought, Structuralism, which focused on understanding the nature of consciousness. This line of thinking is very true to the quest of natural philosophers who sought to understand the nature of things by examining their basic elements in a holistic manner. Again, we are reminded of the dueling inclinations of their predecessors, the philosophers. Wundt chose to understand the more rational and speculative nature of the mind, while James focused on its practicality and usefulness in a function, the operation of the mind. Unhappy with both approaches, a young physician ventured out on his own to create a new school: psychoanalysis.

Sigmund Freud and the psychoanalysts comprised the most influential school of Western thought in the 20th century. Freud (1856-1939) is famous for his psychotherapy technique, *free association*, and his first book, *The Interpretation of Dreams* (1889). It was during his training as a psychiatrist that the seeds of his theory were planted. Freud showed early inclinations towards boldness and risk-taking in his thinking by advocating cocaine for pharmaceutical benefits. The consequences of this idea were monumental, including the addiction of his close friend. Unlike

Functionalism and Structuralism, Freud's theory focused on the unconscious, believing that people are motivated by urges and drives that lie outside of their conscious awareness. Through free association Freud sought to uncover the conflict between norms of the conscious self and unconscious urges that are incompatible with these norms. Although derived from hours of clinical observation of patients, in Freud's work, we see again a dimension of speculative theorizing akin to the natural philosophers. True to their nature, groups of psychologists voiced opinion against introspection and theories of the unconscious as methods appropriate for study of the mind. Through this dissatisfaction, a more empirical method of study arose: Behaviorism.

Like their empiricist fathers, the Behaviorists wanted to study behavior in a manner that they could observe through the senses and test in a more scientifically rigorous manner. Neither introspection, which relied on patients diligently recording information, nor free association, which relied on the physician recording the thoughts of the patient, provided a platform for rigorous scientific study in the tradition of what was now the accepted scientific method. Behaviorism forever changed the practice of psychology and dominated the field for 50 years. The roots of Behaviorism can be traced to American psychologist Edward Lee Thorndike. Thorndike conducted animal studies to determine how long it would take a cat to learn to open a cage to obtain food. From these learnings, Thorndike proposed the *law of effect*, which states that positive rewards will stimulate recurring behavior and negative rewards will extinguish behavior. On the heels of Thorndike's work, Nobel Laureate Ivan Pavlov would identify what is now known as *classic conditioning*. Remembering back to freshmen year psychology, Pavlov conditioned his dogs to salivate at the sound of a ringing bell by associating the ringing bell with receiving food. Further research showed, as we will discuss in later chapters, that people develop preferences and fears through various forms of conditioning. Example is one thing, vision is something else, and up to this point, Behaviorism had examples but no vision.

That changed in 1913 when American psychologist John Watson published a landmark paper titled *Psychology as the Behaviorist Views It*. In this paper, Watson, an animal psychologist at John Hopkins University, set out the vision for Behaviorism. Psychology, he argued, was the study of human behavior; and like animal behavior, it should be studied under strict laboratory conditions. With the embracing of Behaviorism, the science, called psychology, adopted the scientific methods of other sciences and a strict empirical approach to studying the mind, by observing behavior. With this, scientific laboratories flourished across the US with the mission of predicting and controlling behavior. One of the prominent leaders in the field was B. F. Skinner, who coined the term, *reinforcement*. Skinner identified a number of basic learning principles and claimed that they explained the behavior of animals as well as humans. Part of this claim was that nearly all behavior is shaped by the complex relationships to the pattern of reinforcement in a person's environment. These ideas were later used in America to modify behavior in the workplace, the classroom, the clinic, and other settings. Consequently, the impact of his ideas had a profound effect on American society.

A minority of psychologists felt disinclined to adopt the views of either the Psychoanalysts or the Behaviorists. In the work of both groups, they sensed a void that did not address the many dimensions to human existence. From these ideas, the Humanists evolved, focusing on man as an individual with the right to be treated as such. The two most well known Humanists are Carl Rogers and Abraham Maslow. The views of both psychologists are very relevant to our context for belief, and their theories will echo throughout many chapters of this book. Rogers promoted self-centered theory focused on man's desire to satisfy his total self. Rogers stresses that in the development of an individual's personality he strives for "self-actualization (to become oneself), self-maintenance (to keep on being oneself), and self-enhancement (to transcend the status quo)." Maslow, of course, proposed a hierarchy of needs where the individual strives for self-actualization. The very well known self-help book, *Born to Win*, discusses in layperson terms the ideas of Transactional Analysis, focusing on the roles we adopt in dealing with others, principally parent, child, and adult. This is another dimension to the Humanistic tradition. These ideas have demonstrated great resiliency, particularly in expounding the "why" and "how" of human behavior. But none of these approaches addressed what was still an open question for philosophers and some psychologists: How does man come to know? The field of cognitive psychology was born to re-address this unfinished business.

One dimension to cognitive science centers on the notion of our mind as an information processor. Back in the day when the computer was a nascent invention, the analogy between the two was appealing for scientists who sought to understand various unconscious mental processes: how we recall information, how we store information, how we use information, and how we acquire information, all functions which are performed by a computer.

As a result, much like examining the functions of a computer's hardware, cognitive scientists set out to understand certain mental processes. The outcome was a view of our thinking selves that was emotionless. Even though this view has recently changed, there still remains much work to be done. As such, our travels conclude with a quick look at the ostracizing of emotion.

The Ostracizing of Emotion

In the ten years since Daniel Goleman's book, *Emotional Intelligence*, the implications and awareness of ignoring emotions has penetrated global society rapidly. We now are very familiar with words like amygdala and fear conditioning. But, just 20 years earlier, emotions were neatly tucked away in our society. Many adults over the age of 35 grew up believing in the superiority of reason over emotion. Emotions have been viewed as dangerous, unpredictable, unnecessary, and unwarranted. Crimes of passion are given special status over crimes of reason. The rational man has always stood for well-thought out and considered judgment and levelheaded thinking. Thus, while our emotional intelligence has finally received a boost, the totality of emotional life has only recently come to our full awareness and attention. Our increasing awareness stems from the work of neurologists, such as Antonio Damasio, who helped us understand that appropriate reasoning requires emotion, and emotion scientists, such as Joseph LeDoux, who thoughtfully communicated the totality of our emotional life in his work the *Emotional Brain.* Even setting these and other wonderful works aside, using our "common sense" psychology it is hard to think of life without emotion. Nonetheless, at one-point psychologists believed that we would one day look back on emotion as an intellectual curiosity.

Intellectual curiosities or not, our "common sense" psychology also tells us that emotions influence beliefs, but we don't totally understand how and why. Neither do scientists currently working in this area. While the effects of cognition on emotion have received attention, the reverse has not occurred until recently. The result has been our one-dimensional and co-dependent view of belief that does not reflect actual experience or our current knowledge. These perceptions, as we discussed earlier are directly related to philosophers and psychologists historically unfavorable view of emotion. In this section, we examine the "ostracizing of emotion" to understand the events leading up to our modern day context.

It should be stated at the outset that not all philosophers felt that passion was subordinate to reason. Hume famously declared, "Reason is, and ought to be the slave of passions." As well, Kant insisted, "Nothing great is ever done without passion."

Nietzsche celebrated the darker, more instinctual, and less rational motives of the mind. He praised the passions as themselves having more reasons than reason. Beyond these and other few and brief moments of respect, emotions were seen as a burden to rational man.

For the most part, emotions in philosophy related strictly to Ethics. Almost all philosophers relegated the function of emotion to a mere feature in the conduct of human life. Objectively, however, to place philosopher's reason-emotion hierarchy in perspective, we need to look at definitions. Despite use of the word passion in various texts as synonymous to emotion, this is not always necessarily the case. The primary explanation for this is that defining "what is emotion?" is not a simple matter. Its meaning has altered dramatically over the years as theories sway from one direction to the next. So too is the case for the word passion. It has a long and varied history. In some instances an emotion is viewed as one type of passion. Descartes saw emotion in this way. Passions were "perceptions, feelings or emotions of the soul which we relate specifically to it, and which are caused, maintained, and fortified by some movement of the [animal] spirits." Animal spirits, as described in *On the Passions of the Soul*, are minute particles of blood that bring about emotions and related physical effects on the body. Descartes conceived of emotions as very disturbing passions. Hume also advanced a theory of emotion. In the second part of *A Treatise of Human Nature*, he presents notions of emotion presaging problems that scientists would only begin to consider and articulate centuries later.

Given these definitional issues, philosophers chose prudence over speculation and the rationality of reason over the irrationality of emotion, as they saw it. From this perspective, emotion's first and best function seemed to lie in the domain of Ethics, where it could preside over man's treatment of man. Recounting the chronological opinions of the various philosophers is of little benefit; thus, we will spare you the sometimes—unflattering—detail. The turning point for emotion occurred when psychology broke away from philosophy, and the subject of emotion went with the psychologists. It is here that genuine neglect of emotion occurred.

As the science of psychology matured, it, as philosophy had done earlier, began to expand into more and more topics of investigation. Subject areas evolved to assess almost every aspect of human mental functioning: learning, motivation, memory, intelligence, personality, mental disorders, perception, genetics, social behavior, child development, and language. Attacking the complex nature of the human mind lent itself logically to breaking that complexity down into manageable components. What was not so logical was how to re-assemble the findings from these diverse investigations back into a coherent explanation of a human being. To an extent, this is one of the biggest problems psychology and psychologists face, and cognitive psychologists fell into this trap along with their intra-science colleagues.

A second problem for cognitive scientists is the approach they choose to study the mind. Recall that in its infancy psychology divided into two domains, functionalism and structuralism. Cognitive scientists further limited their ability to construct an integrated view of the mind when they chose to investigate the mind functionally. Under the functionalist banner, they elected to work initially only on the hardware of mental life and not to worry about the software. Now, what exactly does that mean, and why is it relevant to emotions? Functionalists care about the *how* of something, not the *why*. They can explain in intricate detail the inter-workings of a thing: How many components it has, what it is made of, what its capacity is, how components work together, and on and on. Why the thing had to be structured in the way it was, however, is not their concern. So, in a computer the hardware components consist of: the motherboard, the memory, the processing chips, the video card, the hard drive, the modem, data storage devices, etc. Our minds also consist of hardware components: memory, language, perception, learning, etc. This is the stuff cognitive scientists worked on: mental functions within the domain of the cognitive unconscious. John Kilstrom coined the phrase to denote the subterranean processes that consumed cognitive scientists. Unconscious processes span a wide variety of mental activities, including the routine analysis of stimuli by sensory systems, remembering, speaking grammatically, imagining, making decisions, as well as forming beliefs and taking action on beliefs. Emotions, however, are considered *conscious* mental states; as such they were considered outside the purview of cognitive study.

Within this definitional environment, emotions were cast outside our cognitive being, ostracized from the other hardware that comprises our mental

life. Once again, the philosophic idea of mind as a
place of logic and reason carried the day.

Are We There Yet?

When one considers history, we should be in awe
that we have gotten as far as we have with emotions
or beliefs. Despite near neglect and subordination
to reason, emotion has managed to find supporters.
And, it is only through their continued interest and
persistence that emotion now has a rightful place
alongside reason in its key roles of thinking, feeling,
consciousness, wellbeing, and surviving. Although
philosophers set out to help us understand the basis
for justified belief, these efforts were encumbered
by their own mental processing biases, and in many
ways, they lost sight of issues central to belief, such
as *why* we choose to believe. While our journey to
understand our modern day context for belief has
ended, our work is just beginning. We know now from
hence we came. Our task from here is determining
"where we are" and "how do we beneficially use
what we've learned?" These questions are answered
throughout the remainder of this book.

CHAPTER 4

Self: Preparing to Become

From A Personality to a Whole Person

Prince Edvard, in the movie *The Prince and M*e, is the kind of person people love to hate: rich, spoiled, reckless. Edvard's character is the direct heir to the Danish throne and wishes, every day, that he did not have to face the pressures that await him. He works tirelessly to avoid these pressures with loose women, fast cars, gambling, and other implied hedonistic pleasures. The problem is, he is bored with them all.

After once again disappointing his parents, during an important meeting to prevent a National Strike, Edvard decides to run away from the responsibilities that await him. On a whim, he enrolls in an American university. Without his parent's financial support or approval for the idea, he gains entry to the university and begins life as a student prince, anonymously.

Initially, the seemingly freewheeling style of American college life seems exactly the distraction that Edvard is seeking. Unfortunately, as Edvard soon learns, life without parental or economic support is not so easy. What had been fun and games quickly turns into serious business when his life collides with Paige, an ambitous pre-med student, who gets stuck with Edvard as an Organic Chemistry lab partner. But, determined, he uses his instincts to obtain employment, befriend Paige, and figure out a way to survive.

What Edvard eventually learns from Paige, like how to work together, becomes invaluable. He even gets to show off his true competencies of racing and Shakespeare. Still, as Paige states during her final exam for a Shakespeare class, "Destiny is not something you can fight against." And, soon, Edvard's destiny beckons as his father becomes seriously ill.

More prepared to face his role, Edvard returns to Denmark. Fearlessly facing the challenges that he had earlier bemoaned, he wins his father's approval to marry Paige and averts the National Strike. Symbolically, as he had earlier promised his father, he proudly and confidently assumes the throne as King, having finally completed his journey to become a whole person.

The Prince and Me is about Paige following her destiny to become a doctor, but equally important, it is about Edvard becoming a whole person. By learning to survive, using instincts, working together with others, expecting successful outcomes, and facing his fears, the young prince learns to be comfortable with his purpose in life, a purpose he did not choose. By managing to grow from the personality he wanted to be, he evolved into the person he needed to become.

Many of us struggle with this choice to remain as we are or fight to become who we could be. We begin examining this cycle of becoming in this chapter, which is written in two parts. The first deals with the initial stage of personal growth: developing our temperament. The second, which comes after the four remaining characteristics of purpose have been discussed, completes our understanding of how we develop "the self" we become.

I appreciate that this format may be confusing. Yet, its flow mirrors our process of becoming. We start with our basic personality structure and a desire to be what we are, as Edvard did. As we learn, grow, and evolve, meanings begin to have context and relevance that contribute to defining the self and, in many, create a yearning to be what we could become. Similar to the evolution that Edvard went through, this cycle includes: learning to work together to survive; acting "as-if" we exist in the world we are trying to create; using our instincts to accomplish the things we need to; and facing the fears that threaten our desire to become. At some point, we do become. While the journey is not an easy one, it is a satisfying one. It starts with developing our temperament.

The Beginning of Self: Temperament

Mysteries of the mind have always stood as one of science's greatest challenges. Housing an entire warehouse of various systems, the mind provides no shortage of mysteries. The normal working mind provides one set of challenges for science. When abnormalities of the mind occur, they ironically provide not only challenges, but also significant clues that help solve some of the mind's mysteries. More than one hundred fifty years ago, science was presented with a challenge that helped provide a potential solution to one of the mind's interesting mysteries.

Phineas Gage, like many men of his day, worked to help construct part of America's railway system.

Proficient and quick thinking, he was a young "up and comer" with the Rutland & Burlington Railroad. Gage had responsibility for several men, and they looked to him for guidance. Stocky and athletic, his crew saw him as one of the ablest amongst them.

Construction work, any construction work, is dangerous. Blasting through hardened stone to lay railroad tracks probably ranks among the most dangerous. Gage, however, was known for his keen concentration, especially in regard to detonations. Yet on one particular day, in one split second, one wrong movement caused a terrible accident. The dynamite that Gage was packing ignited accidentally and sent an iron rod flying straight at him. Forces from the explosion caused the rod to enter and exit Gage's brain leaving a hole from his left cheek to the top of his head.

Miraculously, he was not killed. Nonetheless, something within Gage did die. After a lengthy recovery, his personality was totally different. Once an able-bodied supervisor, Gage was transformed into a wandering derelict. He engaged in odd and even offensive behavior, without any sign of remorse. No longer able to be relied on, he wandered from job to job, lacking direction or purpose. Part of Gage was surely dead. What caused him to lose his sense of social decorum and ability to make appropriate life decisions?

Even a one hundred fifty year old mystery cannot deter a scientist in search of answers. This question and others were obviously too important to go answered. Neurologist Antonio Damasio has spent much of his life seeking answers to what happened to

Phineas Gage and neurological patients like him.

What is it about the brain that causes us to lose part of "who we are" and become someone totally different? The idea of personality is ages old, but our understanding is improving through neurology. In this section, we look at the mind and the individual's temperament, but we add a slight twist. The discussion will combine, when possible, neurological and affective information to help us better understand why we are the way we are. It will also tie into the discussion that we just covered on belief. As I have mentioned numerous times, purpose is about the individual so this is a necessary step in our learning process. Temperament helps us understand how individuals use belief differently to interpret meanings, categorize concepts, modulate seeking, and realize self-esteem. It also helps us understand how different people derive knowing and believing. Lastly, it gives us clues to understand how knowledge is reflected through self-identity. We begin with a bit of background information.

Temperaments exist as a means for the mind/body to functionally use sensory data necessary for the creation of self. Personality develops through experience but is moderated through our temperament to form a balanced, societally-adjusted human being. The notion of temperament makes sense, when viewed from a biological perspective. Our body, and our mind, constantly work to seek balance; this is what homeostatic process is all about. When the body is thirsty, we seek water. When the body is hungry, we seek food. The mind, being part of the body, has the same requirement for balance. This is achieved through two psychological functions, working in conjunction with two attitudinal dispositions. Like everything else in the world, balance is created when the functions and attitudes cooperate through opposite pairing.

Some attack the idea of temperament on the basis of individuality. I read this as an emotional, belief-based reaction: to accept such a proposition is for some a denial of self. But, a simple non-technical demonstration using the CMYK color-scale illustrates why belief in self as a unique individual need not limit our amenability to the notion of temperament. Consider the graphic below.

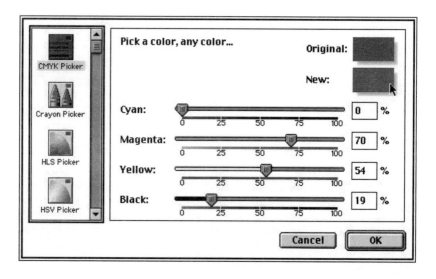

In the CMYK scale, there are four primary colors, just as there are four mental processing mediators. Each increment on the color scale represents a slight variation from the purest Cyan or Magenta to the dullest. To create a color, any color, tiny increments of these four colors are combined. When we consider the number of possible increments, the number of possible color combinations reaches into the trillions, so do the number of possible variations of individuals. Each individual is unique. The combining of the psychological functions, differences in genes, and experiences assures that. Yet, we are each pre-wired to operate within a range of psychological functioning that helps us manage within societal environments. When imbalances occur, mental and emotional disorders result.

The theory of temperament and character has a long history. While I would love to devote time to what I find fascinating background information, I think we are better served sticking to what is really important. There are, however, three individuals who I need to briefly introduce to you: Galen, Karl Jung, and Isabel Briggs-Myers.

Each of these individuals contributed uniquely to our understanding of temperament. Galen was a noted physician of ancient Greece who developed one of the earliest notions of temperament. His theory centered on the notion of bodily fluids called humors. Each humor related to a particular temperament. Karl Jung wrote *Psychological Types*, which explains psychological functioning based on mental preferences. Jung was a protégé of Sigmund Freud, but later in life broke away to develop his own ideas. Jung spent many years of his life articulating the nuances of type behavior, but never developed a framework to make practical use of his theories. Working to fulfill her mother's dream, Isabel Briggs-Meyers used Jung's theories to create a framework for the use of type. She created an inventory that allowed people to determine their psychological type. Like me, she was not a scientist or researcher, yet her determination to help people use this information to understand their differing gifts led to adoption of a Typology Inventory in the late 1950s called Meyers-Briggs Type Indicator. In combining their collective contributions, we use this knowledge to help us understand how temperament effects belief and contributes to defining purpose.

Isabel Briggs-Meyers had great hope for the use of psychological types. As she saw mental preferences as differing gifts, her greatest wish was that her inventory be used to help people identify what they could be best at given their unique gifts. Individual strengths and challenges are determined based on how our mind processes varying forms of information. To illustrate how the mind does this, try the following exercise. Stand up placing your feet shoulder length apart. Next, stretch your arms out vertically, shoulder height. Hold your head up so that you are looking straight ahead. Now push both arms away from the center of your body simultaneously. If you are like most of us (meaning not ambidextrous), you feel a competing force as each arm fights to accommodate your request.

The reaction you experienced is termed "mental processing dominance." One preferred mental process is dominant while the others are positioned in a pecking order. In mental processing mode, the mind naturally defers to the dominant process while an auxiliary process provides balance. In the exercise above, you tried to force your mind to balance two competing signals, which, without lots of practice, it cannot easily accomplish. Consequently, lower level auxiliary complements of mental processing are sparingly used. From this natural tendency of deference to a dominant/auxiliary pairing, we each derive our differing gifts. Likewise, this is also how we innately acquire our challenges, through sparse use of lower level auxiliary processes. Nevertheless, the recognition of dominant-auxiliary functioning drives our desire for personal growth. And, it has been shown that more natural use of each mental process is achievable. As we will discuss later, plasticity (learning capability) of synapses facilitates our ability to enhance our natural abilities and improve in areas where our abilities are naturally limited. Continually pushing the envelope, using our auxiliary functions, is a part of becoming to derive the self. So, let's discuss how we use mental processing.

Using Concepts to Become

The world is full of "things" for lack of a better term. How does our mind go from simply being aware of things to the perception of what these things are or could be? Our ability to conceptualize facilitates the mind's movement from awareness to perception. The mind facilitates conception in numerous ways. One way the mind does this, as we discussed earlier, is by categorizing: grouping things that are alike or that we "qualify" as being alike. To categorize, we look for connections between things. We assess the qualities of various apples or the function of modes of transportation. By assessing how some things are like other things, we create groups. To define the things in those groups, discernible elements about them must be deduced. Paper, or paper-like things, can be deduced into a thing from a group of things that can be marked on. Cars can be deduced into a thing from a group of things that moves other things about. Of course, to make these groups, using their discernible elements, we need a means to formulate connections and evaluate them to make deductions. Finally, as we constantly become aware of new things the methodology of connecting, deducing, and formulating occurs over and over again. Does the mind consider each new occurrence on its own merit or is it somehow influenced by previous occurrences?

Mental Preference Opposite	Mental Process	Mental Preference Opposite
Extraversion (E)	Concept Connectedness	Introversion (I)
Sensing (S)	Concept Interpretation	Intuition (N)
Thinking (T)	Concept Processing	Feeling (F)
Judgment (J)	Concept Sensory Influence	Perception (P)

© Leaps of Thought LLC 2005

The four mental processes and their opposing preferences are presented above. Jung described the Psychological Types more than 80 years ago to communicate how individuals use their minds to manage the process of conception. The next section discusses how these mental processes operate to help us conceptualize and determine meaning in the things around us.

Extraversion—Introversion Preference

In describing the Psychological Types, Jung struggled to find adequate terminology to describe the essence, importance, and pervasiveness of the introvert-extrovert attitude. Jung saw introversion and extraversion as the most relevant aspect of our mental processing because it makes direct use of our feelings.

As we attempt to make sense of and engage the world around us, we make the connection to what we are trying to interpret by reflecting on our feelings. Our "acted-out" sense-making during this connection reflects how we engage and process (using thinking and feeling) sensory concepts within the world. For extroverts and introverts these feelings emanate from different sources. The introvert probes inwardly for direction and guidance. Conversely, the extrovert looks outward in the world about him for direction and guidance. These differing vantage points for interpreting what we perceive lead to differing ways of creating context and meaning, even when an introvert and extrovert interpret the same object.

This is consistent with the finding of Antonio Damasio who asserts, "Through either innate design or by learning, we react to most, perhaps all, objects with emotions, however weak, and subsequent feelings, however feeble." This is further reflected in the work of Turhan Canli, who reports that women who scored high on extraversion had greater brain activity when shown positive external stimuli, such as happy couples, puppies, ice cream, and sunsets. The associations were observable in several areas of the brain that control emotion, including frontal cortex, amygdala and anterior cingulate. Thus, the theory of type and ongoing research implies that whether we are introverted or extraverted plays a key role in how we derive and interpret meaning. Meanings derived during mental processing feed into our sensory structures that form knowledge and beliefs.

Sensing—Intuition Preference

Sensing and Intuition reflect how broadly or deeply we choose to interpret the world of things. Consider the following humorous story taken from *Archimedes' Bathtub* by David Perkins.

> The story is told of the student of physics who faced this problem on an exam.
>
> *Explain how you can use the barometer to measure the height of a tall building.*
>
> The student gave the following answer:
>
> "Take the barometer to the top of the building, attach a long rope to it, lower the barometer to the street, and then bring it up, measuring the length of the rope. The length of the rope is the height of the building."
>
> The answer the professor wanted follows:
>
> "At the top of the skyscraper, the air pressure would measure lower than at the bottom. The difference in air pressure would allow one to calculate the height of the building."
>
> However, the student had explained how to *"use the barometer to measure the height of a tall building."* The problem stated in question. The professor puzzled over how to handle the rebellious response. Another professor was brought in as judge,

and the student was asked to retry the problem, being sure to show knowledge of physics. The student provided the following answers:

"1. Take the barometer to the top of the building, and lean over the edge of the roof. Drop the barometer, timing its fall with a stopwatch. Then using the formula $S = 1/2at^2$ (which says distance fallen equals one-half the acceleration of gravity, times the square of the time elapsed), calculate the height of the building.

2. Take the barometer out on a sunny day and measure the height of the barometer, the length of its shadow, and the length of the shadow of the building, and by the use of simple proportion, determine the height of the building.

3. Take the barometer and begin to walk up the stairs. As you climb the stairs, you mark off the length [vertically, using the barometer] and this will give the height of the building in barometer units.

4. Tie the barometer to the end of a string, swing it as pendulum, and determine with great accuracy the value of g (the acceleration of gravity) at the street level and the top of the building. From the difference between the two values of g, the height of the building can, in principle, be calculated.

5. Take the barometer to the basement and knock on the superintendent's door. When the superintendent answers speak to him as follows: Dear Mr. Superintendent, here I have a very fine barometer. If you will tell me the height of this building, I will give you this barometer..."

The student was given full credit for his answers.

There are many lessons that can be learned from this story, but I would like to make a simple point. A Sensing person sees the world through actualities: A barometer measures air pressure and the difference in air pressure is used to calculate the height of the building. While on the other end of the continuum, the Intuitive person sees the world through possibilities: a barometer is a variable that can be used in many different ways to calculate the height of the building; thus, the student's numerous correct answers. When we categorize, things can be interpreted in different ways. Some people choose to categorize along very strick lines based on elemental attributes of things. Others see very subtle and not so subtle shades of grey in those attributes that don't make them as clear cut as they might appear. Jung noted one of the key issues people in general have with the idea of intuition. It is an unconscious process. Occurring principally in the mind's eye of the Intuiter, the concepts that result from attributes being interrogated in this mental process are not always easy for people to accept or understand. Even the Intuiter himself does not always understand the connections that have traversed his mind to arrive at a concept. Damasio explains how this works:

> "The explicit imagery related to a [an] outcome would be generated, but instead of producing a perceptible body-state change, it would inhibit the regulatory neural circuits located in the brain core, which mediate appetitive, or approach, behaviors. This covert mechanism would be the source of what we call intuition, the mysterious

mechanism by which we arrive at the solution of a problem *without* reasoning toward it."

The difficulty in understanding the intuitive mind is that the process occurs covertly making it difficult to reflect on all of the steps in that process. When the Intuiter steps back into conscious processing mode, they can sometimes logically explain the process for existing concepts. For new conceptions, generally they cannot. When a new concept is being created, all the steps—logical connectors—are not defined at the level of consciousness. Some of steps—connectors—remain hidden in the unconscious. The conscious has made use of this information because it is occurring within the hippocampus knowledge structure. This brain region is a super-convergence zone that integrates information from various brain systems like our emotional and procedural memory.

This possibly explains why Intuiters have great difficulty obtaining acceptance of their concepts. However, as we will discuss in later chapters, the reluctance to take these leaps of faith limit our realization of breakthroughs. As we will learn, breakthrough problems are not amenable to solution through linear reasoning alone. To derive meanings, we need to learn ways to trust our inner voices that help guide us during the cycle of becoming. And they also work to keep us out of harm's way.

Thinking—Feeling Preference
At various points in our conceptualizing effort, the things we have accumulated are assessed for relevance. Although our memories serve as storage

devices, they cannot store everything. And the storage of some things is clearly more important than others. Our thinking and feeling functions mediate our storage and retrieval process through meaning. These are personal and highly subjective. Meanings are derived over time through experience, belief-based and knowledge-based processing, and encoded into our emotive neural sensors as discussed earlier. As we are biologically constructed to seek meaning, the more experiences we record, the better our thinking and feeling functions get at deriving meaning.

Meanings for Thinkers and Feelers are stored in different brain regions and used in different ways. Feelers' object processing is dominantly emotion-based and meanings are assessed using procedural and emotional memory. Thinkers' object processing is dominantly knowledge-based and meanings are assessed using declarative memory. Both types, however, use emotions to signal potential consequences of an outcome, as Damasio's research demonstrated.

Still, the notion of thinking and feeling functions needs to be clarified. To think rationally, we require emotions. Moreover, for us to consciously process emotional signals, feeling is necessary. The logical question that we should be asking then is how can some people derive meanings using feelings and others not? Remember, of course, that mental processes are opposing preferences. One preference is frequently used and the other not.

When the feeling function is preferred, emotion signals are actively used and the resulting feelings more readily interpreted. As object processing occurs in the striatum and amygdala, the activities are more subconscious and less accessible and not easily explainable, similar to intuition.

The thinking signals (from knowledge-based processing) are used sparingly, making them less refined when compared to Thinkers. But the active use of emotional signals gives Feelers the source of their creativity and compassion. Because they are more aware of their emotional signals, more feelings rise to the level of consciousness and get articulated and used routinely. They may also be less inhibited, as they focus less on rationality.

When thinking is the dominant preference, processing is grounded in perceived actualities. Object processing occurs in the hippocampus where processing is slower and more conscious. Processing focuses on the actualities and/or possibilities to become an actuality, making the derived meaning more easily communicated and interpreted. Thus, Thinkers' derived meanings are communicated in what appears to be a more rational and analytical manner.

Derived meanings from Thinkers will have a more concrete and practical tone in their presentation, having been strongly influenced by knowledge-based processing. Feelers' derived meanings will have a natural sense of environmental sensitivity that transcends the perceived actualities around them. Although, there are biases toward one mental processing mode versus another, in reality, both are valid and reliable.

Judgment—Perception Preference

Over a lifetime, many different kinds of individual meanings will be accumulated. How do existing meanings influence potentially new meanings? The

Judgment/Perception attitude determines how much new versus existing sensory influence we use in our decision-making.

Like extraversion and introversion, judging and perception are attitudes, not functions. This means it is a tendency to adopt a certain stance rather than a way of functionally addressing concept processing. When judgment is preferred, new meanings are assessed but need to change the outcome significantly to strongly influence a decision. Using perception (which is a terrible name choice for a descriptor), meanings are constantly given full consideration, sometimes to the point of creating indecision.

Belief-based processing plays a role when either attitudinal disposition is engaged. For the perception attitude, this feeds back into knowledge-based processing to continue the decision-making process. This slows down decision-making because, as Damasio found with his patients, emotional meaning ultimately helps form decisions. Because meanings continually get kicked back to knowledge-based processing mode, they get analyzed and re-analyzed. A decision is not made until there is a necessity (i.e., an overriding meaning) to do so. For the judgment attitude, belief-based processing drives and expedites decision-making. This speeds the decision-making process, but can also cause information to be overlooked in the process.

On the unfortunate day of his accident, Gage's mental processing balance was destroyed. Yet, this tragedy allowed us to discover the neurological mechanisms in the brain that allow us to anticipate the future, decide on the course of action most advantageous for survival, and have a sense of responsibility towards others. A critical clue to solving this mystery lay in understanding the role that emotions and feeling, used in belief-based processing, play in mental processing, particularly decision-making. This was the mystery that Damasio and his team at the University of Iowa College of Medicine uncovered. The descriptions of the mental processing preferences highlight this requirement.

In a healthy brain, these preferences combine to create temperament. We define temperament as an arrangement of inclinations. It reflects a pre-disposition to act in a certain manner. My brother's dog is an English Cocker. For centuries, cockers have been used in bird hunts. When a killed fowl is located, they perch next to it and howl. Recently, my niece dropped a bird-like object from her dresser. The dog immediately ran to the object assumed his perch position and howled, just as he is pre-disposed to do. All creatures, including humans, have pre-disposed tendencies. As mentioned earlier, these tendencies allow us to develop in a manner consistent with the survival requirements of our environment. Gage's behavior prior to the accident reflected the characteristics of a well-adjusted temperament. After the accident, those characteristics no longer existed.

Concept interpretation serves as the anchor to temperament. When we encounter new "things," these things must be interpreted to assess meaning and relevance. This is crucial for survival. Interpreting preferences (Intuition or Sensing) combine with either concept processing (Thinking or Feeling) or concept influencing (Judgment or Perception) to derive the temperament of an individual. Each combination produces a different kind of personality, characterized by interests, values, needs, and habits of mind.

Preference Opposite	Mental Process	Preference Opposite
Sensing (S)	Concept Interpretation	Intuition (N)
Thinking (T)	Concept Processing	Feeling (F)
Judgment (J)	Concept Sensory Influence	Perception (P)

© Leaps of Thought LLC 2005

Through temperament, differing tendencies are created. These tendencies moderate our actions. To give you an idea of how this works, I have briefly described some of the behavioral tendencies of each temperament. While the descriptions are generalizations, as they should be, the individual, based on his or her synaptic connections and somatic markers, uses the pre-wiring of the functions in ways that help them derive meaning and understanding.

SJ Temperament (~ 40% of the American population)

SJs might be considered the individuals that represent the conventional moral fabric of a society. They value law and order, security, propriety, rules, and conformity. Conservative in their views, they are not likely to question authority, buck the chain-of-command, or disregard hierarchy. Responsible and dependable are good adjectives to describe them, as they take responsibility very seriously and are not likely to start something that they cannot commit to finishing. Facts are preferred and used to further the goals of business enterprises they represent. For them, the world is mostly black and white, and they strongly resist delving into grey matter. They run the risk of being slow to adapt and at times appear quite inflexible.

SP Temperament (~ 30% of the American population)

SPs focus on what is occurring in the here and now. They concentrate on assessing the current needs of the situation and addressing it without ado. Structure and rules stifle their need for spontaneity and freedom. Not afraid to take risks, they are enterprising, adventurous, out-going, adaptable, and practical. They have no vested stake in tradition and are willing to adapt in response to changing conditions and circumstances within the environment. While they don't necessarily prefer to play around in the world of the abstract or theoretical, their adaptability allows them to see the practical side of most things. This ability helps them quickly determine practical usefulness, which can influence their willingness to adopt a new idea. Predictability is not a key trait for this temperament. Because they keep their options open, they do not always respect commitments and deadlines are fungible.

NF Temperament (~ 15% of the American population)

The highest point in Maslow's hierarchy of needs is self-actualization, and the NF temperament works continually to get there. Philosophically and spiritually guided, they are constantly seeking the meaning of life. They place high value on integrity and authenticity in people.

Compassionate and giving, they make it their duty to help others grow, and they are very good at it. They use their creative talents to develop solutions and often become the driver for positive change. Their warmth and natural ability to draw out the best in others makes them great motivators. In groups, they work well at resolving conflict and helping others work together to achieve common goals. They have difficultly remaining detached and removing their personal feeling from decision-making processes. At times, they become overly idealistic and fail to see the practical side of a situation.

NT Temperament (~ 15% of the American population)

If the NT temperament could be described in a word, it would probably be "independent." This temperament values its independence and is proud of it. They are the mad scientists driven to excellence, tough on others and even tougher on themselves. Possibilities excite them and consume them. In problem solving they can see solutions from many different perspectives and thrive on the complexity that surrounds ambiguity. With an ability to derive solutions to varying types of problems, they easy fit the role of architects of change. NTs have great vision and the ability to innovate. They easy gravitate to complex theoretical ideas and are strong at deducing principles and trends. Living too closely to the world of complexity makes them difficult to understand. They are deeply skeptical and have no issue with challenging rules, hierarchy, or authority. Often lost in their own world of ideas, they appear insensitive to the needs and issues of the others.

Pscyhological Types have also been described at an organizational level. In *Character of Organizations*, William Bridges communications how the sixteen Psychological Types manifest themselves through organizational structures.

Some Final Thoughts Before We Close

It was in reading Damasio's book, *Descartes' Error*, that the ideas for this book took shape. After researching a great deal of information on belief, the neurological search Damasio embarked on to understand the Gage's of the world provided me with the missing link to understanding purpose and the beliefs that underscore it.

Damasio's hope is that, through neurobiology, we can better understand human beings and find a better way to manage human affairs. I hope he succeeds. A critical aspect to this understanding lies in acknowledging and celebrating the differences that temperaments, created by our neurobiological structures, represent. At the same time, we must understand the limitations that our temperaments innately foster within each of us.

What we often fail to understand is that this innateness is only a starting point. It gives us the necessary tools to manage within and interpret the world around us so that, when we desire, we can make the journey to become. Growing beyond our temperament gives us the means to overcome dimensions of belief that challenge that desire. By achieving greater understanding of the subtle distinctions that derive when various belief dimensions are employed through temperament, we acquire the ability to shape the outcomes we desire using the five characteristics of purpose.

Katherine Briggs was correct. Type is a great tool that can help individuals and organizations understand their differing gifts, but there is more. There are also "archetypes." Though Jung's work covered archetypes, his writings were much too dense to be used for practical application. That changed somewhat with the book *Awakening the Heroes Within* written by Carol S. Pearson. When this chapter resumes, we will explore the nature of archetypes and their role in helping us to grow beyond our personalities to become a whole person.

CHAPTER 5

Unity: Let's Work Together

The Necessity of Meaning

In the year 1888, two blizzards gripped and devastated the United States. The first, known as the Schoolhouse Blizzard, occurred in the Great Plains in January. It came unexpectedly on a warm day and caught many off guard, particularly school children in one-room schoolhouses. The second occurred in March.

On March 10, 1888, the day before the storm, temperatures along the Northeast coast were also unseasonably warm and predicted to remain so. While New Yorkers basked in blissful weather, a low-pressure system that extended from Canada down to the Gulf of Mexico was creating storms in two directions. The northern storm was dropping snow in Green Bay, Wisconsin, as a southern storm was dumping rain on St. Louis, Missouri. It was the southern storm's sudden change in direction that caught the Northeast coast unaware. Late in the day, the storm's course shifted toward the Northeast and moved up the Atlantic coast. As the winds shifted, cold air mixed with warm ocean water, and the result was disastrous.

When New Yorkers woke the next morning, what had been overnight rain was now ten inches of snowfall, and temperatures had dropped from warm to frigid. By the end of the day, eleven more inches of snow had fallen. Unabated, the storm continued for 36 hours. When it was over, the National Weather Service estimated that fifty inches of snow fell in Connecticut and Massachusetts, while New York received forty inches. Winds reached forty-eight miles per hour, with forty- to fifty-feet snowdrifts.

The storm and its aftermath left the entire Northeast paralyzed for two days, and resulted in over 200 deaths in the city of New York alone. The blizzard downed power and telephone lines, stranded those who had ventured away from their homes, and made communication with the rest of the United States nearly impossible. Nearly, but not impossible, because one toll line remained open between Boston and New York city.

When Richard C. Notebaert arrived at Qwest Communications, he walked into the eye of a different kind of storm. Qwest is the fourth-largest telecommunications company in the United States. It provides advanced communication services, data, multimedia, and Internet based services. On June 17, 2002, Notebaert became its chairman and chief executive officer. At the time, the future of the company, indeed, its very survival, was in question.

As did the blizzard of 1888, the storm engulfing Qwest came from two directions: financial peril and employee despondency. Now, I have only met Mr. Notebaert once, but one only has to look at his storied background to know that he is a man who understands how to unite people to work together. This is exactly what he set out to do for Qwest.

The one line that kept New York connected to the rest of the world was watched over by several dedicated and determined linemen from the telecommunications industry. One of these heroes, Angus Macdonald, is pictured below in the portrait titled, "The Spirit of Service." In 1888, the industry was a mere 12-years old. Overhead lines were the only means of transmitting voice signals across the network. Had that only remaining line gone down, it could have meant dire consequences for the city of New York. Banding together to work towards a common goal, Angus and his fellow lineman managed, under horrendous conditions, to keep that line open and New York from slipping into deeper peril.

The Spirit of Service has deep meaning for the telecommunications industry. It has been a part of their heritage for over 100 years. As Notebaert searched for a way to connect with the employees of Qwest to rebuild their struggling company, he recalled that painting. In selecting "The Spirit of Service" as the brand to undergrid the company's vision and values, Notebaert found a way to connect Qwest's employees to the one thing that had universal meaning for them: service. In doing so, he challenged them to deliver on a commitment of heritage, a promise that had been made more than 100 years earlier. Qwest's employees, understanding the need to survive and the universal meaning of service in their industry, responded to that challenge, with Notebaert serving as role model.

Not long after arriving at Qwest, he began hearing from the company's network technicians—the people who install and maintain equipment in homes and offices—that they were ashamed to wear the Qwest logo on their shirts. They would wear street clothes to work, put on their branded clothing during work hours, then change out of their uniforms before heading home. They didn't want to be stopped on the street or in the grocery by people who'd make disparaging remarks about the company they worked for.

Notebaert took it upon himself to wear company-branded clothing every day, including weekends, and he encouraged employees to do the same. By wearing the Qwest logo, he reasoned, not only could he demonstrate pride in the company, but when people made comments about Qwest, it was an opportunity to talk about the company's commitment to service and progress.

By the following year, Qwest people were fully engaged in rebuilding the company and its brand. In 2003, the first full year the Spirit of Service was in place, Qwest people spent more than $1 million of their own money on Qwest-branded gear and clothing—

the very thing they were once ashamed of. They were proud again. And, that pride became infectious.

Renewed pride and morale had significant bottom-line impact as well. Employees began going out of their way to find new customers—or proactively suggest new services to existing ones. A program in which employees referred friends and family members to Qwest resulted in $42 million in new sales in 2004. By all measures, the culture of service had taken hold as Qwest employees lived the vision and values implied by the brand.

The Spirit of Service, as visualized in the Angus Macdonald portrait, has particular meaning to the telecommunications industry. I believe Mr. Notebaert, as he searched for a way to connect with his demoralized and disheartened employees, instinctively knew this.

Meanings, when they are universal, unite us when nothing else can. When we share meaning, we share a common language; it doesn't matter what language we actually speak. This is perhaps why facial expressions are universal.

The universalism of meaning has the power to unite us because we need each other to achieve the work, any work, that we must do. We cannot do it alone. And, because we cannot do it alone, we need to trust the people who will join us and the uncertain process that will guide us. Qwest's employees didn't have that trust in the beginning, but over time they learned to. By accepting the challenge to work together to survive, they implicitly agreed to work within a common framework through which they could work together to survive. That framework supported meaning with values and principles that they would all live by to achieve their common goal.

This chapter focuses on how purpose, through common meaning, helps us form values and principles that are necessary to achieve goals and to align ourselves with others who seek to do the same. We begin by examining the ideas of meaning and truth. Further to this, assuming that individuals can derive congruent significance from meaning and arrive at the same perceived truth, organization and culture result. And, they become the vehicle through which purpose is achieved. We examine how the organization, its purpose, and the culture created within it, is sustained by the values and principles adopted. The chapter concludes by examining how culture can be abused through power.

Meaning and Truth

Businesses establish a purpose and set out to achieve it because it supports their well-being and survival by giving them meaning in the customer's eyes. Many, however, fail to create a meaning that connects with the employees who have to deliver it. With the Spirit of Service brand, Notebaert managed to place the customer first, while connecting with his employees, who needed a reason to believe in the future of their company. In some ways, he was lucky. He didn't have to manufacture a meaning that might ultimately be misunderstood, misconstrued, or worse yet, discarded altogether. Most of us have to search for meaning. And, finding it isn't always easy.

The movie, *A Beautiful Mind*, helps us see why. In Hollywood style, we are taken inside the intellectual, emotional, and psychological world of John Nash. Mr. Nash is a mathematical genius who had an idea: create one original mathematical concept for his PhD dissertation.

When we are introduced to Mr. Nash in the beginning of the movie, we are immediately struck by his intensity, shyness, strength and apparent determination. While other classmates were happy to produce ideas that are incremental improvements that lack originality, Mr. Nash was true to his search for an original concept. We watch as he struggled to see the omission or missing connection within countless mathematical and economic theories, and we wonder whether he even knows what he is searching for. But Mr. Nash is undaunted.

Time passes. Mr. Nash does not attend classes because he feels that this is the surest way to dull one's mind of original thought. His classmates all produce some evidence of their work and worthiness of moving to the next level of their placement. Mr. Nash searches. Upon realizing that he would not receive the placement he sought after his studies, he becomes furious with himself having reached an impasse. But, at a particular moment, while engaging in the sport of trying to attract women, Nash had an enlightened thought. With that thought, purpose became clear to Mr. Nash, and purpose—contributions to the concept of Game Theory—won him the Nobel Prize in Economics in 1994.

Meaning is rarely as seemingly clear as the "Spirit of Service" or applications for Game Theory. And please note the words "seemingly clear" in the previous sentence. Clarity is only achieved when relevancy has the same meaning and a desirable outcome for everyone involved, which was one aspect of Mr. Nash's contribution to Game Theory. Yet, as we have learned in earlier chapters, our belief systems and temperament play important roles in how relevance is interpreted, making universal meaning difficult and, sometimes, impossible. This suggests that, more often than not, relevancy takes on many meanings and that those meanings need to be adaptable to the individuals who need to act on them so that they are desirable. To appreciate how difficult it is to create universal meaning for those who collectively need to act on it, we need to understand what happens during appraisal and when perceived truths are being generated.

In chapter one, purpose was defined as meaning: the manner in which we create context from which relevancy can be derived. This is what Notebaert did with the Spirit of Service brand and what Mr. Nash did when he derived the economic principles that underscore Game Theory. In each situation, the context had sufficient relevance to connect with people who could and/or needed to use it to generate actions—actions that supported and maintained their wellbeing. As we discussed in Chapter 2, appraisal is the neurobiological process by which relevance is assessed to motivate action.

Any time we assess the significance of something to us that potentially effects our wellbeing, we make an appraisal. It does not matter whether it is a small thing, like breaking a nail,—which is not so small if you are a hand model—or a big thing, like being diagnosed with cancer. When a stimulus triggers circuits, indicating a potential circumstance threatens our "self-defined idea" of wellbeing, the body begins an emotion-driven process, which includes appraisal, that will result in action. Even if the action is to do nothing, an outcome occurs. In the case of the broken nail, doing nothing implies the action to simply let it grow back, and, in the case of cancer, the action to ignore it implies allowing the body to eventually atrophy and die. In both cases, the action of inaction produces an outcome regardless of whether the intended outcome was arrived at deliberately or passively.

Recall, from our earlier discussion on belief's role in creating meaning, that our self-involved inquiry, while centered on two specific questions, is expressed introspectively in numerous ways. This introspection arises when circuits in our body that process information and store records of prior experiences become active. This triggers activation of emotional signals that generate feelings of benefit or harm and produces a body state that focuses our attention on whether we need to consider the "perceived" truth of a relevant situation. Significance to the individual is raised to the level of consciousness by the resulting feelings. When significance related to our personal wellbeing is detected, no matter how faint, our body begins the process of determining the truth of the relevant situation. Truths take the form of: "I believe or think this will be an outcome for this situation;" "I do not believe or think this will be an outcome for the situation;" or "I do not know what I believe or think will be an outcome for the situation."

These neurobiological activities, assessing meaning for relevance and determining perceived truth, relate to

Antonio Damasio's somatic-marker hypothesis as depicted below.

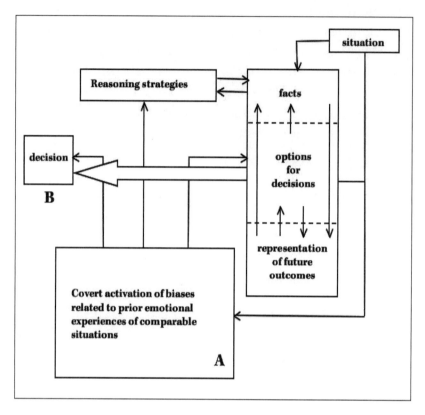

Emotional signaling brings consequences of a situation to the level of consciousness through feelings, helps individuals derive meaning, and, when necessary, act-out desired outcomes related to perceived truth. In *Looking for Spinoza*, Damasio explains how emotional signaling accomplishes this important task:

> Covertly or overtly, it focuses attention on certain aspects of the problem [or situation] and thus

enhances the quality of reasoning over it. When the signal is overt it produces automated alarm signals relative to options of action that are likely to lead to negative outcomes. A gut feeling can suggest that you refrain from a choice that, in the past, has led to negative consequences, and it can do so ahead of your own regular reasoning telling you precisely the same "Do not." The emotional signal can also produce the contrary of an alarm signal, and urge the rapid endorsement of a certain option because, in the system's history, it has been associated with a positive outcome.

Appraisal occurs during the *covert activation* of biases related to prior experiences highlighted in Area A of Figure 5-1. Favorable or unfavorable outcomes are reflected in the perceived truth of the situation, which is sometimes reflected in the *decision*, highlighted in Area B of Figure 5-1. Because we do not always follow the guidance our body signals generate, there is not always congruence between our perceived truth and our actions. As both Damasio and Lazarus have noted, it is possibly our appraisal of significance that is often cited in research related to decisions under certainty.

Before the Spirit of Service brand took root, Qwest's network technicians faced a situation that some interpreted as significant to their well-being: shame in what their organization stood for—poor service. Faced with the decision of whether to believe in the Spirit of Service brand, some employees chose to believe their new situation was true while others did not. Those who believed, or, at least, decided to wait and see, remained with the company. Those who did not believe left, if they could.

For those who believed and remained, Notebaert's action of wearing the company's branded apparel was a validation of their perceived truth (Figure 5-1: Area B). However, it was a crucial step towards adapting the appraisals of those who were undecided. Over time, as employees joined Notebaert in "acting-out" the meaning of the Spirit of Service brand, their emotional experiences of comparable situations changed (Figure 5-1: Area A). For those who were undecided, this enabled changes to their previous biases. In other words, their appraisals adapted from harmful to beneficial assessments of significance. Further, their perceived truth adapted from "I'm not sure this is true" to "This is true or going to be true." This affirmation created an environment where Qwest's cultural transformation could by all measures take hold, as it did.

Unfortunately, appraisals may not have changed for Qwest employees who remained but did not believe their new situation was true. This results from markers' resistance to change as noted in the definition of belief. In the final chapter, we discuss actions organizations can take when employees have difficulty adapting their beliefs.

How we assess meaning to determine relevance and interpret perceived truth is pivotal to choosing whether we will work together with others in achieving a common goal. Once this occurs, we have an organization. Yet, an organization's survival remains questionable until the individuals within it learn to work together. Part of learning is determining how to work together best. As individuals go about figuring this out, principles, rules/methods of working, and value judgments (collectively ideologies) begin to take root. Continuously using and adapting these ideologies creates a set of principles and an informal guidebook emerges for coexistence and cooperation. This unwritten guidebook forms the basis of culture.

Creating Unity through Culture

Culture as formally defined, by Edward Schein author of *Organizational Culture and Leadership*, is "a pattern of shared basic assumptions that was learned by a group as it solved its problems of external adaptation and internal integration, that has worked well enough to be considered valid and, therefore, to be taught to new members as the correct way to perceive, think, and feel in relation to those problems." Business leadership, particularly strategic planning, became interested in culture in the 1980s. This interest was generated as American firms became increasingly aware of the success of their Japanese competitors and concluded that culture possibly played a role in this success. Similarly, as other foreign companies gained market share in industries such as steel, shoes, electronics, and others, the link between culture and competitive advantage could not be ignored. Contradictory though it may have seemed to corporate America's psychological construct, which favors self-identity as an independent rather than interdependent being, it became necessary to understand the competitive advantage of culture and to incorporate this knowledge alongside the dry and overly rational approaches to strategy that dominated business school approaches and, as a result, business thinking at the time. Thus, momentum to use culture building to create competitive advantages for American companies started just twenty years ago. Until that time, and even today, most American companies felt little need to embrace what was considered Asian-style thinking.

In the mid-1960s, before this momentum began, Swedish consultants from the Scandinavian Institutes for Administrative Research spearheaded initial research effort into this area. Two leaders of the Institute, Eric Rhenman, who wrote *Organization Theory for Long Range Planning*, and Richard Normann, who wrote *Management for Growth*, laid the foundation for how consultants that followed thought about, approached, and addressed issues of culture within organizations. Though interest in research areas set off by their insight petered out in the late 70s, their influence has had a lasting impact.

On the other side of the pond, in the United States, industry had progressed in highly sophisticated ways that facilitated systematic research into how and why organizations operate as they do. This early effort was led by Peter Drucker when he wrote *Concept of the Corporation*, which was first published in 1964. Mr. Drucker states: "It was the first book that looked upon a 'business' as an 'organization' that is, as a social structure that brings together human beings in order to satisfy economic needs and wants of a community." Mr. Drucker, considered the Father of the Science of Management, is a writer and management thinker who has consistently been ahead of his time. It often took others a least a decade to catch up to his thinking.

In the area of culture, it took more than Drucker and the collective will of consultants in Sweden. It took sufficient threat from the Japanese to get American management thinkers to react to the issues of cultures. True to the American self-construct favoring an independently-driven organizational being, those reactions were not entirely positive.

Rightly or wrongly, many American management thinkers viewed culture from the same lens that most things are viewed: economics. From this purview, what culture is, how it arises, how it's used, and how it should be changed was and is often hotly debated. This book takes a different point of view. Culture is about one thing: survival of the organized unit. As this is culture's primary functional characteristic, it exists to maintain cohesiveness, strengthen ties, minimize de-stabilization, and deflect uncertainty related to the unit's perceived truth. In others words, it is a nurturing system structured to perpetuate belief in the unit's purpose to sustain survival.

Let's consider, again, Qwest's Spirit of Service brand promise. This was, at its inception, only a promise; it was not a certainty or a reality. In spite of the resonance of common meaning invoked by the portrait, the common actions required to make it a reality were embodied only in the employee's "perceived truth" that they could deliver them. The continuous nurturing of belief in their perceived truth through culture is what allowed Qwest to not only survive but also, ultimately, thrive and transform its environment.

We must accept or at least appreciate that our highly civilized societies allow us to function under the mind-set delusion of absolute truth. As we have already discussed, truth is relative; it is not absolute. Even after we have acted-out our perceived truth to create meaning, as Qwest's employees did, we have not created permanence. As Heraclitus rightly pointed out several millennia ago, there is an unceasing changing of things, and the world is always subject to new modifications.

As the world changes by acting-out of our perceived truths, others who do not believe will create their own worldview, making our truth relative in particular circumstances. Culture ensures that the uncertainty that can and will creep in as we act-out our truth is held at bay by our belief systems programmed to ignore them. Unfortunately, this is, again, a dimension of belief that hinders our need to evolve, once purpose gains transformational momentum. This unproductive stickiness of belief is addressed in the final chapter of the book.

Culture continuously addresses the question: "What are our challenges to achieving purpose/ meaning and survival?" It does this by consciously and unconsciously monitoring the environment, just as nurturing systems within our bodies do. Homeostasis, a fundamental phenomenon within biological systems, is one example. In humans, homeostasis maintains the relative constancy of various bodily processes, such as the delicate balance of sugars and salts, to ensure that cells function and interact with required elements that facilitate survival. Consider what happens when you become ill. The affected cells in the body send healing agents to the required areas. With proper nutrition, the body is best placed to deal with the imbalances naturally. If it cannot, it sends signals to your brain to let you know that other support systems are required. If these support systems arrive in a timely manner, the illness may be treated appropriately and effectively, without significant intermediation. If, however, support systems are not sought until the illness has reached a critical point, significant intermediation will be required and, in unfortunate instances, will not be able to arrest the problem. Thus, while balance is critical to maintaining the strength and stability of the system, it is equally as important that signals and warnings be acknowledged and responded to. Within organizations, culture achieves this. When potential threats to cohesiveness or destabilizing influences occur, culture acts to combat these effects by finding ways to continuously reinforce the prinicples and values that serve as the guidebook to purpose. HP provides an excellent example of how using this guidebook culture maintains cohesiveness, strengthens ties, minimizes destabilization, and deflects uncertainty related to the unit's perceived truth.

In 2003, we watched the very open and bitter battle between Carly Fiorina (then CEO of HP) and Walter Hewlett, son of co-founder William Hewlett, then a member of HP's board. The battle raged over Mrs. Fiorina's goal to acquire Compaq computers. The differences of opinion regarding the merits of the merger ranged from questions over true value creation to issues of culture integration. While Ms. Fiorina won the battle, HP did acquire Compaq; ultimately, HP lost. According to a Washington Post article, in 2004, HP lost significant market share to computer maker Dell, Inc., as the company's share of PC sales worldwide declined to 15.8 percent worldwide from 19.3 percent in 1999. It also lost ground to technology services giant IBM. The merger was supposed to help them become stronger to compete against these two companies. But, she lost, too. In February 2005, Mrs. Fiorina was asked to resign. At the time of her resignation, HP stock was worth 70 percent of what it was when she became CEO and about 90 percent of its value before the merger was announced.

To possibly understand what Mr. Hewlett sensed, here is the background to HP's culture.

Bill Hewlett and Dave Packard founded Hewlett Packard on January 1, 1939, after completing their graduate studies in engineering. They had met several years earlier as undergraduates at Stanford University and became fast friends during a two-week camping trip. From their very first product, excellence in product design that made a discernible difference to the dynamic of business was the hallmark of the company. This belief continues to serve as one of the company's core values to this day. Their first product, an oscillator, was purchased by The Walt Disney Company to enable the screening of Disney's innovative *Fantasia* in 1940. That excellence in product design and acceptance helped turn a trickle of government contracts into a flood. Soon, the company began to grow steadily. While it grew, Dave and Bill planted the seeds that lovingly flowered into HP's culture.

HP is responsible for many cultural "firsts" that many of us now take for granted. After only one year in business, they made their first donation to local charities. Later this charitable giving was formalized into HP views on corporate citizenship. They organized the first company-wide catastrophic health insurance, after an employee contracted tuberculosis. In 1940, profit sharing was introduced where the janitor and the CEO were paid the same percentages.

In business management, Dave Packard's style of walking around talking with employees, getting personally involved, having good listening skills, and the recognition that "everyone in the organization wants to do a good job," was later dubbed by management theorists as "management by walking around." Also, the "open door policy" was established by creating an atmosphere of trust and mutual understanding by having a very open-plan seating environment for everyone in the company, including its two founders. (IBM's early use of an "Open Door" policy is also noted in *A Business and Its Beliefs*.)

Also, in 1948, HP adopted an insured pension plan for all employees with a minimum of five-years service.

When HP went public in 1957, it was the first company to grant stock to employees—out of respect for the worker. All employees at all levels with six months of service received an automatic stock grant and became eligible for a stock option program. Still, as much as they welcomed this continued growth and success, questions of "how" the company should grow were as hotly debated as "how much" the company should grow. To come to a common understanding, the company held its first off-site meeting of senior managers during the year of the IPO. At this meeting, the HP corporate objectives were written. The objectives served as a day-to-day guide for management decision-making. According to Dave Packard:

> "We thought that if we could get everyone to agree on what our objectives were and to understand what we were trying to do, then we could turn them loose and they would move in a common direction."

The objectives of the company cover seven points: profit, customers, fields of interest, growth, our people, management, and citizenship. Once the values were set, HP continued to break new ground in organizational development. In 1959, they implemented a stock purchase plan. In 1967, they pioneered the concept of flexible working hours, or "flex time" at their operation in Boehlingen, Germany. Later in 1973, HP became the first American company to provide flextime for its workers. Bill Hewlett explained that flextime allowed workers "to gain time for family leisure, conduct personal business, avoid traffic jams, or satisfy other individual needs." Further, Dave Packard commented that "to my mind, flextime is the essence of respect for and trust in people."

There are numerous examples of how HP's rich nurturing system, culture, acted unhesitatingly throughout its long history to make HP's purpose work and continue to ensure its survival. In *Built to Last*, authors James C. Collins and Jerry I. Porras shared this story:

"What follows is an actual conversation between a seasoned lab manager and a young product manager at HP in 1984:

Product Manager: "We've got to introduce an IBM-compatible personal computer *now*. That's where the market is going. That's where the volume is. That's what customers primarily want."

Lab Manager: "But where's the technical contribution? Until we figure out a way to make an IBM-compatible personal computer with a clear technical advantage, then we just can't do it—no matter how big the market."

Product Manager: "But what if that's not what customers want? What if they jus want to run their software and don't really care about technical contribution?   And what if the market window will close unless we act now?"

Lab Manager: "Then we shouldn't be in that business. That's not who we are. We simply shouldn't be in markets that don't value technical contribution. That's just not what the Hewlett-Packard Company is all about."

Bill Hewlett's son understood what HP was all about. He also understood the role of HP's culture. Instinctively, he knew the merger would not create the value-enhancing results numerous spreadsheet models—that have no hope of ever capturing culture— told the Board and HP shareholders it would. Yes, HP needs to meet the challenges of the twenty-first century; all companies do. But, the mechanism within their environment that ensures and enables survival was not used wisely to facilitate that process: culture.

When we don't take care of our cultures, we lose the only system available to ensure survival of the corporation. CEOs don't do it alone. Both Hewlett and Packard didn't just know this; they embodied this. When we don't take care of our culture, it can't take care of the organization. One way to severely damage culture is through the abuse of power. Let's take a look at it's damaging effects.

Power: The Abuse of Culture

As the authors of *Strategy Safari* insightfully note: "Power takes that entity called organization and fragments it; culture knits a collection of individuals into an integrated entity called organization. In effect, one focuses primarily on self-interest, the other on common interest." This is a very appropriate starting point for our disucssion.

General Motors (GM) was once king of the automotive industry. It began the early 1960s riding a wave of success that reached its crest under the leadership of Alfred P. Sloan, Jr. Sloan became president and chief executive officer of GM in 1923 and remained with the company as chairman of the board until 1956. Hailed an administrative genius, he turned GM into a model of modern business organization during his tenure. In fact, *Concept of the Corporation* studies the inter-workings of GM's organizational environment during an eighteen-month period that began in January 1943.

During Sloan's stewardship, GM was reorganized from a collection of uncoordinated weak business units into an enterprise consisting of divisions with coordinated activities. Divisions, though supported by centralized functions, retained substantial authority within the organized structure. The "concept of the corporation," as Drucker described it, became a model for organizational design across all sectors of the US economy, both private and public. Culture clearly flourished within this organization as GM led the way in annual automotive styling, sales methodologies, and innovations in consumer financing.

This picture changed as finance gained considerable power throughout the organization. As vice chairman Elmer Johnson recalls:

> "Finance exerts a tremendous dominance over our entire organization. I'm not just talking about the number of our chairmen that have been selected from finance but the degree to which finance infiltrates all of our other functions. Our head of personnel is from finance, our head of public affairs is from finance, heads of Pontiac, Buick and Oldsmobile as well...Over time this has led to us becoming fixated on volume (and revenues) at the sacrifice of other considerations."

Power destabilizes an organization when it becomes so concentrated that it drowns out signals culture was meant to communicate when problems (i.e., threats to survival) loom on the horizon. In GM's case, not listening to and adjusting its actions to heed these signals resulted in the company becoming unresponsive and unable to adapt to changes in the marketplace. In HP's case, the power resided in one individual, Carly Fiorina, but the result was them same: the company's performance suffered. Beyond this, finance's stranglehold on GM's culture limited its effectiveness in deflecting uncertainty of the organization's perceived truth. As continued experiences of failure or mediocre performance replaced prior successes, new biases and resulting appraisals emerged over time. These adapted appraisals did not go unnoticed. Particularly during the 1980s, as foreign firms became formidable competitors, GM lost its automotive styling leadership, patents declined, and top-flight executives left the company. By the early 1990s, a substantial number of plants in the US closed and tens of thousands of workers lost their jobs. Had GM's Sloan-inspired culture not been completely stifled as a result of power some departments might have successfully minimized finance's destabilizing actions.

The nuturing system of culture comes together to create. The values and principles necessary to guide the day-to-day actions of that creation are selected because they help structure and place boundaries around what will be created: a new environment. Our next characteristic of purpose, expectations, explores how the organization goes about enacting that environment.

CHAPTER 6

Expectations: The Enacted Environment

The Enacted Environment

John Lennon said: "Imagine all the people living life in peace." In *Pleasantville*, they didn't have to imagine, they lived a life of peace and tranquility. The sun always shines, the grass is always green everyone always smiles, problems are easily resolved, and the high school basketball team never loses. It was a world of perfection.

The people of Pleasantville had lots of expectations. Bud's dad, Mr. Parker, always expected dinner to be prepared when he arrived home from work; people were expected to smile and say "hello" when they met each other on the street; though the library held books, no one was expected to read them; and, while there were roads, no one was expected to travel beyond Main Street. Each and every day, the characters of Pleasantville "acted-out" their world. With that acting-out, their expectations were continually self-fulfilled. There was only one problem with Pleasantville; none of it was real.

Pleasantville is a TV world of perfection. To achieve their enacted environment, its citizens suppressed important aspects of their true selves. When their true nature or hidden nature was exposed, their enacted environment changed in many ways, good and bad. This chapter focuses on how purpose fuels expectations to create outcomes by examining their role in helping us enact our environments, for better and for worse. We examine why "acting-out" is a necessary part of enacting, and how our belief systems encourage and support this.

Why We Act-Out

Purpose drives our want, need, desire, and determination to achieve. We saw it quite clearly as John Nash searched patiently and determinedly for his one original concept. And as with Mr. Nash, purpose is the impetus that starts the creation cycle. To this point, our discussion focused on the actualities essential to the characteristics of purpose: temperament, personal significance, relevance, meaning, and truth. Now, let's consider purpose in the abstract.

Purpose has two components: vision and passion. Working as a unit they drive our creative, inventive, and imagining capabilities and are supported by our belief system. As the driver of creating, purpose causes actions to occur; however, those actions may or not be coordinated or even performed with conscious intent. It is not until these actions become deliberate and organized that they begin the start of a conscious vision. Until that time, purpose is simply an inadequately used and undirected drive swirling around inside our heads, as depicted with John Nash.

Once this drive achieves direction from personal significance, relevance, meaning, and perceived truth, purpose serves as a unifier— as with Notebaert and Qwest employees—binding together the actions of those who believe the resulting vision to be true.

So, what triggers vision? Let's see.

Purpose is a desire or need that builds up inside us when we believe that a fundamental change has to or will occur or a problem must be solved. At some point, needs become expectations. Unlike discrete changes that we make in our goals, when we believe fundamental change has to happen or a problem must be resolved this thought becomes pervasive in our thinking. The more the belief is reinforced through sensory experience, the more it becomes ingrained. Reinforcement facilitates the shift from a desired outcome (i.e., a need or want) to an expectation that becomes the catalyst for something that we never knew, but imagined, should be a permanent feature of our life. This expectation forms a driving vision.

"Expected" environments brought to life occur when individuals who connect through personal significance, relevance, meaning, and perceived truth begin acting out this vision. Essentially, we make-up actions consistent with the world we mentally create. In business, we call this "executing strategy," as individuals we call this "life."

History is littered with stories of these connections, which evolved from expectations that became driving visions within individuals to shared visions amongst a group: Martin Luther King, Jr. and the Civil Rights Advocates; Thomas Edison and his research assistants; Moses and the enslaved Jews; Gandhi and the formerly-colonialized Indian nation; and Henry Ford and the U. S. autoworkers. Each of these individuals and groups had expectations about how the world should be or could be. Those expectations connected with the expectations of many others and, ultimately, became shared visions. Rosa Parks's expectation of equality connected to the expectations of others, and together their driving visions became a shared vision, which was the Civil Rights Movement. Rural workers' expectation of earning a better living than they could through agrarian employment connected with Henry Ford's expectation that every man could own a car to create the United States Automobile Industry. It is easy to see how the creation of individual visions can connect to become a shared vision, and it is with shared visions that we, over the centuries, have propelled our societies to achieve the seemingly unachievable. Higher education is a good example.

Creating and developing the modern university free of religious influence, structure, and teaching started out as the invention of a German diplomat and civil servant, Wilhelm von Humboldt. In 1809, he became Prussian minister of education, and one-year later conceived and founded Friedrich Wilhelm University (now Humboldt University in Berlin). His expectation for education in Germany was to demonstrate clear leadership in scholarship and research and education that was accessible to many. By 1840, it had done just that. The university could boast of 1,750 enrolled students; being world renowned for its modern curriculum; an impartial and nondogmatic spirit of intellectual inquiry; and specialized scientific research.

Sixty years on, Humboldt's idea of the university as a change agent was picked up in the United States. In 1870, the United States had no more than half the college students it had had in 1830 even though the population had tripled. In the next thirty years, a range of American university presidents created and built a new "American University," which had previously imitated the German model that promoted the Prussian idea of academic freedom and supported the goal of education for the many. With impetus from the Morrill Act of 1962, growth in colleges tripled over thirty years. The US gained worldwide leadership in scholarship and research, having founded leading institutions during that period such as Massachusetts Institute of Technology and Cornell University.

After World War II, a new generation of American academic entrepreneurs, with new expectations for their world, anticipated a different vision for education in America and worked together with others to build "private" and "metropolitan" universities. These universities made a significant contribution to growth in American higher education since World War II. Though these new schools differed little from older institutions in the curriculum, they served a new student "market" that had very different needs.

This new market was for older, rather than young adults directly out of high school; it was for city students commuting to the university at all hours of the day and night rather than for students living on campus and going to school full time; it was also for students from diverse and heterogeneous backgrounds. Basically, these new schools enacted an environment by creating to a new student population. They also shifted the status of the college degree from "upper class" to "middle class." Ultimately, a new expectation arose about what going to college meant. This shift created middle class society in the US, as we know it today.

This shift in education expectations arose from the visions of post-World War II American academic entrepreneurs. They sensed the changing nature of learning and social demographics—growth in American industry, growth in city living, changes to student demographic profiles, and a myriad of other issues. As they acknowledged and responded to the changes around them, they learned and, as they did, their expectations for the future of urban education began to take shape. These expectations utltimately began to drive their vision, which connected with others to create a shared vision. And, by acting-out this vision, they enacted a new world of education in a manner that enabled others to participate in and benefit from its creation.

We greatly benefit from expectations that turn to visions when they become actualities that enhance societies' wellbeing, individually or collectively. Thus, given their importance to enacting our environments, let's explore this mental phenomenon in more detail.

Expectations as Self-Fulfilling Prophecies

In chapter one, we discussed Sony's expectations for the future. Psychologically, their feeling served as evidence of their ability to overcome challenges and achieve goals, and fostered their expectations. Termed the "feelings-as-evidence" hypothesis, studies in the area explain why things we feel experientially are taken as valid and serve as confirmation of our beliefs. Examining this hypothesis in more detail helps us begin to understand why expectations become self-fulfilling prophecies.

Emotional feelings possess two important attributes: they

provide information and they guide attention. Strong emotions initiate attentional funneling—a feedback loop that narrows attention to goal-relevant information. As discussed in chapter 5, they also provide information about the appraisal of situations that relate to personal relevance and concerns. Through feelings, information about appraisals can be accessed privately. Publicly, feeling becomes accessible through body language, which shares with others pain, frustration, excitement, and hope. It is the experiential nature of feeling that contributes to our ability to derive personal significance from situations.

This is supported by research results demonstrating that information value is the most important aspect of an experience. When focused on performing a task or solving a problem, feedback about performance often comes via our feelings. Such is the case for example when we "feel" good about an answer on an exam. During such events, we monitor our beliefs, expectations, and abilities to determine whether our performance is adequate or whether we need new information. We make assessments on the basis of the feedback our feelings provide. This process leads to our continuous reliance on beliefs and expectations as predictors of future outcomes for similar or related circumstances.

As we go about experiencing and creating our world, we attempt to match our subjective and objective information. Like a hurricane that gains momentum as it progresses, strong beliefs about something will elicit strong feelings, and strong feelings will elicit a search for supporting evidence. Achieving affirmation of the belief makes the feeling stronger and continues the cycle. The feedback cycle our feelings and beliefs engage in sets up "feelings-as-evidence."

According to Gerald L. Clore and Karen Gasper, authors of *Feeling is believing: Some affective influences on belief:* "Cognitive and affective feelings, despite the fact that they are self-produced, may be experienced as internal evidence for beliefs that rival the power of external evidence from the environment."

In Sony's case, when they began, feelings were vital, as they went about trying to figure out the new world around them—an action we call "sensemaking." After all, there wasn't much else: there was hope, 1600 yen, 20 eager colleagues, a dismal work area, passion, a vague vision, and values. For them to continue building a world that did not exist, they had to act-out and, as a result, enact the world they sought to create.

Enacting is crucial to creating. Before something is enacted (i.e., created together) the world is effectively a glob of ambiguous things that represent our experience. The environment is created as our human interactions and actions make sense out of those things. This sensemaking feeds into our information processing that supports appraisals and determines meaning. Sensemaking, as defined by Karl E. Weick, is

"the enlargement of small cues. It is a search for context within which small details fit together and make sense. It is people interacting to flesh out hunches. It is a continuous alternation between particulars and explanations, with each cycle

giving added form and substance to the other. It is
about building confidence as the particulars begin
to cohere and the explanation allows increasingly
accurate deductions ... Whatever coherence such
a process has derives in large part from one of two
structures: beliefs or actions."

Because we are biologically organized to search for
meaning, we create relationships between things and
bring connections and patterns to our actions that are
consistent with our sensemaking, which temperament
facilitates. As we create relationships and draw lines
to things, events, and objects, situations begin to
become meaningful and have relevance in the eyes
of those we enact our world with. But, it should be
clear from the previous chapter, not everyone is
included in that world. Nonetheless, sensemaking
starts the information gathering process that leads
to expectations. Fueled by feelings-as-evidence and
enacting, these expectations become self-fulfilling
prophecies.

That expectations become self-fulfilling prophecies is
not new. There have been many research experiments
in this area. The most well-known study titled
Pygmalion in the Classroom was conducted in the
1960s. In this study, children were randomly selected
as targets. Their teachers were then informed that
these students had been identified by a fictitious study
called the "Harvard Test of Inflected Acquisition" to
excel in intellectual performance over the next eight
months. Eight months later, some students achieved
significant gains in scoring, but only the students who
had been identified to do so by the research team.

In *Successful Intelligence*, Robert J. Sternberg recounts his own story of expectations. When Sternberg was an elementary school student, they were required to take IQ tests. From the sounding of "Go!" to start the exam, he dreaded every moment of the examination. While other students beavered away through page after page, he was still working on the first page of the exam. Since how quickly you can respond to questions to provide an answer is a measure of intellignce,—because someone said it was a long time ago—the resulting low scores Sternberg received set his teachers' expectations. Just as "scoring" had positively set the expectations of the teachers in the Pygmalion project, his teachers expected nothing from him. And, he gave them exactly what they expected.

Fortunately for the rest of us, his fourth grade teacher didn't allow an IQ test at the age of nine to set his or her expectation. Now Dr. Sternberg, he is the IBM Professor of Psychology and Education at Yale University. He has a BA from Yale, a PhD from Stanford University and four honorary doctorates. As Dr. Sternberg reached to overcome low expectations, we have all benefited from his triarchic theory of intelligence and his work into the nature of insight. Having started life as a student who could have entered "the twilight zone," as he calls it, he works to help us better understand the nature of intelligence. As Hume pointed out several hundred years earlier, expectation is not knowledge, though we constantly treat it as such. If we truly want to get our heads around how meaning and thinking ability create intelligence, the influence of expectations has to be considered and addressed. Thinking critically about these influences, it should not be surprising that our use of "feelings-as-evidence" driven by belief is one reason expectations like these become self-fulfilling prophecies. Moreover, the simple fact that we act-out our expectations to enact our environment is another. Let's consider how this happens.

From Expectations to Enacted Environments

That enactment is a by-product of expectations doesn't seem particularly surprising. After all, expectations stem from beliefs. *Born to Win* is a perennial best seller that discusses how expectations transfer, particularly, from parent to child, and how these expectations set us up to fail or succeed in life. Recently, I read a commencement speech given by Steve Jobs to the June 2005 graduating class of Stanford University. His story is a powerful one because it demonstrates how expectations set the course of our lives; but also, how, through sensemaking, we can use this knowledge and learn to enact our world free of expectations that might have otherwise come to define us. We conclude this chapter with his story.

For those of you who don't know, Steve Jobs is the CEO of Apple and Pixar Animation Studios. Not only is he the CEO of Apple, he also co-founded it. At Stanford's graduation ceremony, Mr. Jobs shared three life stories:

> I dropped out of Reed College after the first [six] months, but then stayed around as a drop-in for another 18 months or so before I really quit. So why did I drop out?

It started before I was born. My biological mother was a young, unwed college graduate student, and she decided to put me up for adoption. She felt very strongly that I should be adopted by college graduates, so everything was all set for me to be adopted at birth by a lawyer and his wife. Except that when I popped out they decided at the last minute that they really wanted a girl. So my parents, who were on a waiting list, got a call in the middle of the night asking: "We have an unexpected baby boy; do you want him?" They said: "Of course." My biological mother later found out that my mother had never graduated from college and that my father had never graduated from high school. She refused to sign the final adoption papers. She only relented a few months later when my parents promised that I would someday go to college. And 17 years later I did go to college. But I naively chose a college that was almost as expensive as Stanford, and all of my working-class parents' savings were being spent on my college tuition.

After six months, I couldn't see the value in it. I had no idea what I wanted to do with my life and no idea how college was going to help me figure it out. And here I was spending all of the money my parents had saved their entire life. So I decided to drop out and trust that it would all work out OK. It was pretty scary at the time, but looking back it was one of the best decisions I ever made. The minute I dropped out I could stop taking the required classes that didn't interest me, and begin dropping in on the ones that looked interesting.

It wasn't all romantic. I didn't have a dorm room, so I slept on the floor in friends' rooms, I returned coke bottles for the 5¢ deposits to buy food with, and I would walk the seven miles across town every Sunday night to get one good meal a week at the Hare Krishna temple. I loved it. And much of what I stumbled into by following my curiosity and intuition turned out to be priceless later on.

Let me give you one example: Reed College at that time offered perhaps the best calligraphy instruction in the country. Throughout the campus every poster, every label on every drawer, was beautifully hand calligraphed. Because I had dropped out and didn't have to take the normal classes, I decided to take a calligraphy class to learn how to do this. I learned about serif and san serif typefaces, about varying the amount of space between different letter combinations, about what makes great typography great. It was beautiful, historical, artistically subtle in a way that science can't capture, and I found it fascinating. None of this had even a hope of any practical application in my life. But ten years later, when we were designing the first Macintosh computer, it all came back to me. And we designed it all into the Mac. It was the first computer with beautiful typography. If I had never dropped in on that single course in college, the Mac would have never had multiple typefaces or proportionally spaced fonts. And since Windows just copied the Mac, it's likely that no personal computer would have them. If I had never dropped out, I would have never dropped in on this calligraphy class, and personal computers might not have the wonderful typography that they do. Of course, it was impossible to connect the dots looking forward when I was in college. But it was very, very clear looking backwards ten years later. Again, you can't connect the dots looking forward; you can only connect them looking backwards. So you have to trust that the dots will somehow connect in your future. You have to trust in something - your gut, destiny, life, karma, whatever. This approach has never let me down, and it has made all the difference in my life.

My second story is about love and loss. I was lucky – I found what I loved to do early in life. Woz and I started Apple in my parents' garage when I was 20. We worked hard, and in 10 years Apple had grown from just the two of us in a garage into a $2 billion company with over 4000 employees. We had just released our finest creation—the Macintosh—a year earlier, and I had just turned 30. And then, I got fired. How can you get fired from a company you started? Well, as Apple grew we hired someone who I thought was very talented to run the company with me, and for the first year or so things went well. But then our visions of the future began to diverge and eventually we had a falling out. When we did, our Board of Directors sided with him. So, at 30, I was out. And very publicly out. What had been the focus of my entire adult life was gone, and it was devastating. I really didn't know what to do for a few months. I felt that I had let the previous generation of entrepreneurs down - that I had dropped the baton as it was being passed to me. I

met with David Packard and Bob Noyce and tried
to apologize for screwing up so badly. I was a very
public failure, and I even thought about running
away from the valley. But something slowly began
to dawn on me – I still loved what I did. The turn
of events at Apple had not changed that one bit.
I had been rejected, but I was still in love. And
so I decided to start over. I didn't see it then, but
it turned out that getting fired from Apple was
the best thing that could have ever happened
to me. The heaviness of being successful was
replaced by the lightness of being a beginner
again, less sure about everything. It freed me to
enter one of the most creative periods of my life.
During the next five years, I started a company
named NeXT, another company named Pixar, and
fell in love with an amazing woman who would
become my wife. Pixar went on to create the
world's first computer animated feature film, Toy
Story, and is now the most successful animation
studio in the world. In a remarkable turn of events,
Apple bought NeXT, I retuned to Apple, and the
technology we developed at NeXT is at the heart
of Apple's current renaissance. And Laurene and
I have a wonderful family together. I'm pretty sure
none of this would have happened if I hadn't been
fired from Apple. It was awful tasting medicine,
but I guess the patient needed it. Sometimes life
hits you in the head with a brick. Don't lose faith.
I'm convinced that the only thing that kept me
going was that I loved what I did. You've got to
find what you love. And that is as true for your
work as it is for your lovers. Your work is going to

fill a large part of your life, and the only way to be truly satisfied is to do what you believe is great work. And the only way to do great work is to love what you do. If you haven't found it yet, keep looking. Don't settle. As with all matters of the heart, you'll know when you find it. And, like any great relationship, it just gets better and better as the years roll on. So keep looking until you find it. Don't settle.

My third story is about death. When I was 17, I read a quote that went something like: "If you live each day as if it was your last, someday you'll most certainly be right." It made an impression on me, and since then, for the past 33-years, I have looked in the mirror every morning and asked myself: "If today were the last day of my life, would I want to do what I am about to do today?" And whenever the answer has been "No" for too many days in a row, I know I need to change something.

Remembering that I'll be dead soon is the most important tool I've ever encountered to help me make the big choices in life. Because almost everything—all external expectations, all pride, all fear of embarrassment or failure—these things just fall away in the face of death, leaving only what is truly important. Remembering that you are going to die is the best way I know to avoid the trap of thinking you have something to lose. You are already naked. There is no reason not to follow your heart.

About a year ago I was diagnosed with cancer. I had a scan at 7:30 in the morning, and it clearly showed a tumor on my pancreas. I didn't even know what a pancreas was. The doctors told me this was almost certainly a type of cancer that is incurable, and that I should expect to live no longer than three to six months. My doctor advised me to go home and get my affairs in order, which is doctor's code for prepare to die. It means to try to tell your kids everything you thought you'd have the next 10 years to tell them in just a few months. It means to make sure everything is buttoned up so that it will be as easy as possible for your family. It means to say your goodbyes. I lived with that diagnosis all day. Later that evening I had a biopsy, where they stuck an endoscope down my throat, through my stomach and into my intestines, put a needle into my pancreas and got a few cells from the tumor. I was sedated, but my wife, who was there, told me that when they viewed the cells under a microscope the doctors started crying because it turned out to be a very rare form of pancreatic cancer that is curable with surgery. I had the surgery and I'm fine now.

This was the closest I've been to facing death, and I hope it's the closest I get for a few more decades. Having lived through it, I can now say this to you with a bit more certainty than when death was a useful but purely intellectual concept: No one wants to die. Even people who want to go to heaven don't want to die to get there. And yet death is the destination we all share. No one has ever escaped it. And that is as it should be, because Death is very likely the single best invention of Life. It is Life's change agent. It clears out the old to make way for the new. Right now the new is you, but someday not too long from now, you will gradually become the old and be cleared away. Sorry to be so dramatic, but it is quite true. Your time is limited, so don't waste it living someone else's life. Don't be trapped by dogma - which is living with the results of other people's thinking. Don't let the noise of other's opinions drown out your own inner voice. And most important, have the courage to follow your heart and intuition. They somehow already know what you truly want to become. Everything else is secondary.

When I was young, there was an amazing publication called The Whole Earth Catalog, which was one of the bibles of my generation. It was created by a fellow named Stewart Brand not far from here in Menlo Park, and he brought it to life with his poetic touch. This was in the late 1960s, before personal computers and desktop publishing, so it was all made with typewriters, scissors, and Polaroid cameras. It was sort of like Google in paperback form, 35 years before Google came along: it was idealistic, and overflowing with neat tools and great notions. Stewart and his team put out several issues of The Whole Earth Catalog, and then when it had run its course, they put out a final issue. It was the mid-1970s, and I was your age. On the back cover of their final issue was a photograph of an early morning country road, the kind you might find yourself hitchhiking on if you were so adventurous. Beneath it were the words: "Stay Hungry. Stay Foolish." It was their farewell message as they signed off. Stay Hungry. Stay Foolish. And I have always wished that for myself. And now, as you graduate to begin anew, I wish that for you. Stay Hungry. Stay Foolish. Thank you all very much.

Mr. Jobs's words of inspiration illustrate clearly how expectations, sensemaking, and acting-out work interdependently to help us enact our world. Yes, expectations set us up for better and for worse, but we don't have to choose to live those expectations. Mr. Jobs choose to not "act-out" his biological mother's expectation of him being a college graduate. While he clearly understood the importance of education, something inside him rejected his mother's definition of what that meant. In doing so, he found a way to gain education and knowledge without the limitations her expectation placed on him. Although, Mr. Jobs dropped out, he didn't opt-out. He was still a student, simply not in the traditional sense of the word. By re-defining "dropping-out" by informally "dropping-in," what is normally deemed to be failure wasn't at all. It was an opportunity to learn based on what seemed to have personal relevance and significance to him. As we have already discussed, through this personal significance we create meaning. The art of calligraphy had meaning for Mr. Jobs. That meaning became obvious as the Macintosh was being created.

Further, what computing and technology meant to Mr. Jobs was seriously tested as he struggled to deal with the loss of his role at Apple. During that time, the lessons learned at Reed University about continually searching for meaning in the things you love were invaluable. Often things in our lives just don't make sense. They seem to not have comprehensible meanings, and we just don't understand them. At these times, acting-out so that we can enact the environment we seek helps to make sense of a situation. Creating NeXT allowed Mr. Jobs to enact a new vision for computing and software and, in time, make sense of his world, again. Like Mr. Jobs said, we can run away. He thought about it. In fact, that would probably have been the easy thing to do. He had lots of money, so he didn't have to opt back in. Yet, he did. And, by doing so, things that didn't make sense before began to make sense, and there are two flourishing companies to show for it.

Having given him up, Mr. Jobs's biological mother wanted to set him up for success. Many people expect that a college education will do that. For his own reasons, Mr. Jobs thought otherwise. He thought it was more important to follow the path his sensemaking (i.e., gut instincts) routed out for him, even when it didn't make sense. By doing so, he found out what he loved and determined what had meaning, and the rest followed. He urged Stanford's graduates to do the same.

The World as We Would Like To See It

In 1985 the article, *Strategic Management in an Enacted World*, was published by authors Linda Smircich and Charles Stubbart. In it they presented the view that strategic environments are enacted through the social construction and interaction processes of organized actors. Numerous authors in interpretative sociology have echoed a similar message throughout the years:

"Organization members actively form (enact) their environments through their social interaction. A pattern of enactment establishes the foundation of organizational reality, and in turn has effects in shaping future enactments. The task of strategic management in this view is organization making— to create and maintain systems of shared meaning that facilitate organized actions."

Just what social interaction, shared meanings, and organized actions are enacted depends entirely on the organization and/or the individual. Steve Jobs found a way to enact an environment that has meaning for him. The most important thing was not to settle for something he didn't love. We should all demand no less for ourselves.

In the next chapter, we discuss a very important innate mental faculty used for sensemaking and act-outing. As Hume pointed out, expectations, just as belief, become so tightly woven into our mental processing that it is difficult for us to think about them as anything but absolute truths. They form habits of thinking that lock us into seeing and responding to the world. Expectations are so compelling that we are even willing to shut out reality to live this truth, as the citizens of Pleasantville did. While this convenience of certainty aids us in the routine and rudimentariness, it hinders us in the creation of the new. Without the courage and wisdom to address the limitatons of expectations, Apple and Pixar would not exist. Steve Jobs mentioned several times in his speech the impetus behind this: his instincts. By trusting his instincts, Jobs was able to break with patterns of the familiar, created and molded by others' expectations, to invent the new. We now begin to delve more deeply into our inner drives to learn how instincts help us create the new by achieving goal-desired outcomes that make purpose work.

CHAPTER 7

Instincts: The Magic of Improvisation

Creating What We Sense

On March 2nd and April 22nd, 1959, Miles Davis and several of the world's best jazz musicians came together and would later make history. That history in the making was the recording of *Kind of Blue*, the greatest selling jazz album of all time. Improvisation at its best was achieved on that occasion.

The musicians on the recording included: Bill Evans on piano; Wynton Kelley on piano for Freddie Freeloader; Paul Chambers on bass; and the legendary John Coltrane and Cannonball Adderley on saxophone. Four decades on, *Kind of Blue* is the premier album of its time, irrespective of musical genre. Deeply engrained in our psyche as the essence of cool, its piano and bass opening is instantly recognizable the world over. If one only has one jazz album, it is most likely *Kind of Blue*. And, if one only knows one jazz musician, it is probably Miles Davis. *Kind of Blue* represents one of Miles's most innovative contributions to the world of jazz. For that contribution, jazz fans of all ages reward him by continuing to pay homage through album purchases. As Ashley Khan, author of *Kind of Blue: The Making of the Miles Davis Masterpiece*, notes, "In the church of jazz, Kind of Blue is one of the holy relics."

What makes *Kind of Blue* special is not only its musical impact on the world, but how the music came to be. Recorded at Columbia's 30th Street Studio, which was a church, each complete performance was a "take," in modal form, with the scales scribbled out on scraps of paper. Basically, in a sense, it was an experiment in new jazz forms.

Modal jazz was not the musical style predominately used by musicians at the time. Chord progressions were, and the two styles differ greatly. Modal jazz is played using musical modes that represent the seven scales used in medieval music. Modes were "rediscovered" by composers like Claude Debussy and frequently used by 20th century composers.

When *Kind of Blue* was recorded, musicians used chords to provide background for their solos, in bebop, as well as in hard-bop, a song would start out with a theme, which would introduce the chords used for the solos. These chords would be repeated throughout the whole song, while the soloists would play their parts. The repetition was frustrating for musicians. Using modes, the bassist, as one example, didn't have to "walk" from one important note of a chord to another—as long as he stayed in the scale being used and accentuated the right notes within the scale—he could virtually go everywhere. Using the modal approach the soloist had more freedom.

According to research by Khan:

"If not entirely unrehearsed or of Davis's composition, Kind of Blue was still a bold step forward for the trumpeter. He was defining a self-reliant, studio-based approach that in 1959, for the first time in Columbia's studio, allowed him to direct a whole project from composing to bandleading and recording. If Miles prepared any written directions for Kind of Blue, they would have been a few motifs sketched on staff paper. Evans remembered that, "Like 'Freddie Freeloader,' 'So What,' and 'All Blues,' there was nothing written out." Davis later admitted: "I didn't write out the music for Kind of Blue, but brought in sketches for what everybody was supposed to play because I wanted a lot of spontaneity in the playing."

And spontaneity is what they delivered. There were no highly structured musical sheets, no rehearsals, no fancy engineering, and no re-takes." As Joe Cobb insightfully noted:

> "To improvise as well as they did, these guys had to have learned a lot from the jazz giants. You get to hear the spirit of all those players in the recording of Kind of Blue."

Kind of Blue's note liner written by Bill Evans eloquently sums up the challenge of jazz improvisation:

> "There is a Japanese visual art in which the artist is forced to be spontaneous. He must paint on a thin parchment with a special brush and black water paint in such a way that an unnatural or interrupted stroke will destroy the line or break through the parchment. Erasures or changes are impossible. These artists must practice a particular discipline, that of allowing

the idea to express itself in communication with their hands in such a direct way that deliberation cannot interfere.

The resulting pictures lack the complex composition and textures of ordinary painting, but it is said that those who see well will find something captured that escapes explanation.

This conviction that direct deed is the most meaningful reflection, I believe, has prompted the evolutions of the extremely severe and unique disciplines of the jazz or improvising musician.

Group improvisation is a further challenge. Aside from the weighty technical problem of collective coherent thinking, there is the very human, even social need for sympathy from all the members for the common result. This most difficult problem, I think, is beautifully met and solved on this recording."

Rising to meet this challenge, the sextet used their musical instincts masterfully on those two days.

This chapter explores the requirement for people to use their instinctive competencies to achieve desired results. Uncommon results are best achieved when people are able to best use their information interpretation skills, which fuel their instinctive competencies. It also improves goal realization efforts. This is the magic of jazz. Everyone does what he or she does best with minimal direction. In business, individuals are rarely allowed to use their innate abilities to craft desired results. This removes context and meaning that would contribute significantly to the busines realizing its objectives. For individuals to attach meaning and context that would improve their instinctive competencies, businesses must achieve greater flexibility in roles, processes, strategies, and responsibilities.

Creating through Improvisation

Blink, Malcolm Gladwell's latest bestseller, explores the art and science of thinking without thinking. This natural ability to allow our instincts to guide us swiftly through decisions where thinking would otherwise take too long or intrude into the process is artfully described in Evans liner notes. Moreover, he captures the damaging effect of deliberately intertwining or interjecting thinking into a process that our senses are highly capable of performing unassisted. The creative process is driven in large measure by our willingness to give ourselves over to that process and allowing our instinctive talents to direct and guide our actions. Throughout evolution, instincts have served us well in the goal of survival.

At some point during the creation of what has now become the corporation, we've forgotten this. The more I think about this, the more it baffles me, because many of the world's greatest insights and most useful inventions were created by accident or by simply letting the process create itself using instincts. Let's begin to understand why.

Ever go to the refrigerator, open it, and then stare at the contents inside? Have you ever gone into a room or place searching for something without knowing what you're looking for? Or, my personal favorite—which I do often—have you ever gone surfing on the Internet looking for something, going from site-to-site looking for something but you have no idea what? Well, needless to say, you are not alone. What your body is doing is seeking. It is looking for something that captures your attention and directs your activities toward some desired (but possibly undefined) goal. Neuroscientists call this drive the Seeking System. And, it is fundamental to survival as well as learning.

In Chapter 5, we talked about the biological process called homeostasis. To refresh your memory, this process maintains the relative constancy of various bodily processes, such as our need for water, to ensure that cells function and interact with required elements that facilitate survival. Our Seeking System is pivotal to the body's autonomous ability to achieve this. But, this system doesn't just make sure that we don't allow ourselves to go hungry. It also ensures that our ability to create through sensemaking and other mental tools is supported by goading us (i.e., provoking action) as we search for meanings. It does this by informing complex behaviors, like searching for knowledge, curiosities about ourselves, and the world around us. Given this role in learning and development, it is foundational to our ability to change, evolve, and grow.

Neuroscience researcher Jaak Panksepp, Distinguished Professor Emeritus of Psychology and Adjunct Professor of Psychiatry at the Medical College of Ohio, discovered Seeking Systems. His experiments involving Seeking Systems, which are not covered in this book, are communicated in *Affective Neuroscience*, which he authored in 1998. In the book, he explains that Seeking Systems "give us the impulse to become actively engaged with the world and to extract meaning from our various circumstances."

Seeking is activated when our bodies activate dopamine synapses in our nervous system. Once activated, dopamine circuits play a critical role in directing our attention. The circuitry does this by deciding what's salient in our environment. According to Dr. Panksepp: "These circuits appear to be major contributors to our feelings of engagement and excitement as we seek the material resources needed for bodily survival, and also when we pursue the cognitive interest that brings positive existential meanings into our lives." Under dopamine's influence, events or thoughts jump out of the background, grab our attention, move us to act, and drive goal-directed behavior. In other words, it's the impetus behind our internal motivation.

Because the release of dopamine is present in all animals, this implies that we are all self-motivated. In following these instinctive drives, we have a higher probability of connecting with things that stimulate our appetitive (i.e., desire) drive. As Dr. Panksepp says: "Without dopamine circuits human aspirations remain frozen. When they are not active, many potentials of the brain cannot readily be manifested in thought or action. When they are active, a person feels as if he or she can do anything." The more "engaging," "stimulating," "eagerly-anticipated," and "life-altering" experiences we have, the more we will seek. That's because having active dopamine circuits makes us feel good. The more dopamine experiences we have, the more we want. Seeking is a way to get them.

Jazz musicians create in an environment where their seeking systems are free to follow their instincts. Most of us do not have that luxury in our work environments. But, a few of us do. Here's an example of one work environment that does: 3M.

3M began life as a mining company in 1902 in the town of Two Harbors, Minnesota. It was formed with the promise of significant venture returns from the mining of corundum, a mineral harder than diamonds, by a group of men who knew nothing about mining. If it sounds too good to be true, that's because it was. As often is the case when loose money chases a quick return on investment, fact and fiction had not been clearly separated.

Without a customer, the company forged ahead to achieve its dream. After two years of learning through the school of hard knocks, the company sold its first batch of minerals. In the life of a start-up, this would be cause for celebration. Except, in this instance, the deposits turned out not to be corundum. What the company had mined was anorthosite, a soft mineral unsuitable for use on grinding wheels—its intended purpose. Without a product to sell and without money, the founders began searching for a way to make the company viable. It was decided that if they couldn't provide the raw materials used in grinding that they would manufacture the grinding wheels themselves, despite lacking knowledge of the business.

They had assumed that they could use the mineral they had mined to make their wheels. Having not researched the market, they were unaware that a young inventor named Edward Acheson, who previously worked under Thomas

Edison, had discovered how to make an artificial abrasive, carborundum, by combining carbon and silicon. According to the National Inventor's Hall of Fame, "without carborundum, the mass production manufacturing of precision-ground, interchangeable metal parts would [have] been practically impossible." Fortunately, the young company soon realized that they were well behind Acheson's learning curve. They abandoned the idea of making grinding wheels and went searching for a new one. This time, they would manufacture sandpaper—another product they knew nothing about.

There's a saying "third time lucky" and, finally, 3M's luck began to change. Lucius Ordway, an outside investor, invested in the company. Though his initial investment was small, it was enough to keep the company alive and moving toward its new objective. Importantly, over the following two years, Ordway slowly increased his investment until it reached $200,000. Even though they had begun to achieve sales, it became obvious that more capital would be required. So, in addition to providing capital the young company needed, he also took the unusual step of becoming its President. In this capacity, he personally approved every purchase and every check issued. Moreover, his sage advice steered the company away from boom-or-bust investments and illegal activities like price fixing.

In spite of these difficult and troubling times, the company continued to be dominated by a spirit of survival. This spirit gave them the perseverance and fortitude to weather the storms that lay ahead.

After much effort and a considerable wait, the

first sand paper products were shipped to customers. Sadly, these were almost the last products they would ship as well. Each day customers sent their product back. The product quality was dismal, and no quality process existed to help them understand what had gone wrong. To add to their troubles, the sales manager charged with dealing with customer complaints quit. In his place, a young bookkeeper, William McKnight was asked to fill the role. Of course, McKnight knew nothing about sales or quality assurance, two problems which required immediate attention. But he believed experimenting gave people a means to figure out problems. So he encouraged his fellow employees to do just that. They began to seek solutions.

Against all hope, they searched frantically to determine what had caused the problem. By accident, a worker dropped the garnet used to make sand paper into a bucket of water. When he reached over to retrieve it, he noticed the water was oily. If oil had gotten on the garnet, it would not adhere to the glue on the sandpaper backing. So, in a painstaking process, each step of the garnet's shipping process was retraced in detail. Yes, the garnet had been exposed to oil as it traveled across the Atlantic Ocean from Spain. Still the good news was they finally identified the problem. Although a solution wasn't immediately apparent, by experimenting, their factory superintendent eventually realized he could cook the oil away by roasting the garnet.

With a solution to the problem identified, 3M focused its efforts on rebuilding its reputation and relationships with customers. Recognizing the talents of their young and dedicated staff, McKnight was promoted to general manager and a new, up-and-comer, Archibald Bush, was selected to lead the company's sales effort. Relatedly, the oily garnet incident led to 3M's first quality program. To ensure that product quality received the attention it required, Bill Vievering became 3M's first quality assurance employee. After numerous false starts, the company had finally found its way.

Fortunately for 3M, throughout their first twelve years of existence, the gods, while not at all kind, were at least merciful. Their harrowing story makes it abundantly clear that the freedom to seek and learn enabled employee's creative and problem solving spirits to flourish. With patience, their efforts were given time to take root and helped the company live to tell its tale. To this day, 3M's willingness to free employees to use their seeking drives in highly productive ways has continuously led to insights and breakthroughs. Let's examine why.

Creating Insights and Learning to be Responsive

Many approaches, frameworks, and strategies have been created to help organizations achieve what is a natural process: evolution. Through evolution, we change and grow, hopefully, into something better. Innovation—the change engine that replaces the old with the new— is the lever within ourselves and companies that enables us to achieve this. But as we just saw with 3M, innovation can't be systematically engineered or created at will. There are simply too many unknown and uncertain forces that we can't anticipate, nor do we need to. That's what our instincts are for. They give us the ability, without prior warning or planning, to deal with the unknown and the unexpected, just as 3M did. So it seems, at least to me, counterintuitive that our activities related to innovation are planned. Not only are they planned; they are managed.

In a process, one can plan. Innovation is not a process. The distinction is subtle but important. Processes begin and end. They have a defined starting point and a defined ending point. Change, which innovation creates, has no starting point or ending point. It is continuous, just as systems are. Systems are interrelated and interdependent connections, like water. Water systems all connect together; there is no start or end. Change is the same. Every change causes a change—an interrelated and interdependent connection. Because innovation is a system, to change one must respond, not plan.

If we consider the nature of uncertainty, it should give us pause long enough to consider or re-consider what it means to respond. And, clearly, what we recently witnessed during the aftermath of Hurricane Katrina yields an easily understood point of reference. Considering the implications of not responding, we'll examine why responsiveness is a natural way to achieve insights, which is a vital part of changing, evolving, and surviving. We'll also see that planning can't duplicate the tortoise and leap frog approach necessary for insights to occur.

At any point in time, systems can become imbalanced and disequilibrium will result. This is equivalent to a pipe that has burst in a water system or a structural crack that has occurred in a building foundation. We know what will happen if the imbalance is not corrected; the system will slowly deteriorate over time and, ultimately, a collapse will occur. Organizations, with or without strong cultures, go through a similar destabilization process. A crack occurs somewhere in the system: loss of touch with customers; inefficient cost structures; too many products to serve a particular market; missed opportunities; and on and on the list goes. To attempt to catch these imbalances, companies create predetermined examinations of the environment to assess weaknesses in the system: it is called the planning process.

The disadvantage of planned processes is their inflexibility in changing course as events unfold. The ultimate planning system was the former Soviet Union, which employed more than 800,000 economists in connection with planning. The country was able to decide on the direction it wanted to set and mobilize huge resources to enable the country to achieve its objectives. However, the rigidity it exhibited, ultimately, led to its downfall as the process was unable to see the necessary changes that were needed in light of changing geopolitical situations. This process makes sense when the world is expected to change slowly and predictably while intended strategies unfold, so that our acting reflects exactly what we planned. Unfortunately, the world and uncertainty don't work that way. We saw this clearly during Hurricane Katrina. Events unfolded, conditions worsened, and people died. As conditions changed rapidly, the plans of FEMA were initially unwavering. Despite the fact that we could see the ineffectiveness of their actions in real-time, the original plans were changed very slowly.

GE, up to the 1980s, was a strong proponent of planning. The complex planning system at GE before the 1980s enabled GE to exert financial control over its vast network of companies. However, it made it difficult to generate new revenue and pursue entrepreneurial opportunities with its core businesses. When Jack Welch became CEO, he recognized the shortcomings of the planning system. As a former division manager, he understood its drawbacks and the restrictive nature. The principal problem is the planners' heavy reliance on data rather than their instincts about observations. When planners get buried in their data, they fail to capitalize on instinctive opportunities when they occur.

Imagine yourself as the captain of a submarine tasked with protecting the environment and watching for changing conditions. Before the voyage your plan is established, and you and your crew follow that plan. Part of the plan involves roles and responsibilities for the crew, and each day you focus on those planned activities and roles. Everyone on the submarine has a role that they perform with alacrity and efficiency. However, certain members of the crew have quite an important role, manning the periscope. To accomplish this as planned, at prescribed intervals throughout the journey, they take turns raising the periscope and observing what occurs in the surrounding environment. If they observe nothing unusual, they lower the periscope, make note of the observations and return to their other responsibilities. Because it's not part of the plan, no one wonders or investigates what has changed when the periscope was not up—

until a potential disaster strikes. Unfortunately, at that point, it's probably too late to wonder.

Granted, this oversimplifies a complex reality. But it gets to the heart of the issue: organizations behave in a manner very similar to the crew of our imaginary submarine. They have the same need to search and monitor for changing conditions, and they accomplish it in the same way, occasionally looking out beyond their desks to observe what is currently occurring in the surrounding environment. And neither the submarine captain nor the organization's CEO is aware of what has happened while the periscope was not lifted as they are both submerged in their environment and its attendant responsibilities. Under these conditions, identifying meaningful insights and creating breakthroughs is naturally hindered within organizations.

The problem organizations face is that planning operates in a manner counter to how uncertainty unfolds and how people within the enacted environments they create search for meaning, seek, and create. Now, let me explain what I mean by that.

Insight is a key determiner to whether we will be caught by or whether we will capitalize on changing conditions and uncertainties within our environment. It is also a critical element of breakthrough thinking.

I need to take you back inside the movie world of Dr. Nash in *A Beautiful Mind* for a moment. As you recall, the movie tells the story of Dr. Nash, his life work and his life struggle. Dr. Nash's discovery of an important economic principle is chronicled in the early stages of the movie. Communicated through various scenes presented below, the director, Ron

Howard, helpfully provides a visual account of the elements of breakthrough thinking. Researchers have found that these elements (or ones similar to them) are commonly present when achieving insights and creating breakthroughs. While they cannot say with specificity how these mental processes occur, they generally agree that they do occur. What follows is an identification of each element of breakthrough thinking along with a brief discussion of the scene as Dr. Nash's moment of insight unfolds on screen.

- *Searching* – Nash searched patiently and persistently for one original idea throughout his doctorate studies while his fellow classmates were content to publish "incremental" ideas. Nash researched many mathematical and economic theories in search of his original idea. There is a particularly amusing scene where he follows pigeons around looking for a pattern.
- *Ripeness* – Nash's searching placed him in a position to see "an analogy which nobody had seen before."
- *Incubation* – Nash reached a crisis in the movie when he learned that he will not receive a place because he has not submitted any materials on his doctoral thesis. Nash conceded to himself that he didn't know what he was looking for and that he's seemingly reached an impasse in identifying a problem statement. At this point, he takes a break with his fellow classmates at the pub.
- *Bisociation/Reframing* – Nash makes an unusual mental connection when thinking

about how he and his friends could each get a date with a group of girls. The problem was, one girl in the group was particularly attractive and several of the guys might want to win her favor. As he tries to assess how to successfully resolve this situation, a different problem statement occurs to him. Through bisociation, the girls are used as an analogy to *reframe* a previously answered problem. Reframing led to the possibly that the previously accepted answer was wrong.

- *Breaking Codes* – In restating the question, Nash discards a widely held premise put forth by Adam Smith that had been the foundation of economics for 150 years, achieving a breakthrough in economic theory in the process.

Arthur Koestler in *Act of Creation* coined the terms above to describe the activities that occur during breakthrough thinking. Other authors have used other terms; however, the descriptive nature of the activities is generally consistent with those of Koestler. I deferred to Koestler's terms because through *Act of Creation* published in 1969, he genuinely set the stage for and provided a great deal of food for thought to later researchers in the areas of breakthrough thinking and insight. I felt it appropriate to acknowledge his groundbreaking work, which is exceptional in its own right because Koestler was not a scientist. He is best described as a journalist, novelist, political activist, and social philosopher. It is a testament to his multi-disciplinary thinking skills that his early insights have withstood the test of time.

These elements or activities work together to help create insights and breakthrough thinking. We cannot say that we know for certain why insights occur, but we have learned from research into the areas of intelligence and creativity that these elements facilitate insights that can change our lives, and others, for the better as well as helping us learn to be more responsive to the need for change.

Responsiveness is, in some respects, built into the elements themselves. Searching is facilitated by our Seeking Systems and innate skills of observation. For us to make the best use of this element, however, we must learn what it means to "search." We have become accustomed to the idea that searching relates to looking for some "identifiable" thing. For things of familiarity, such is the case. If your son or daughter loses a ball, you search for it. If your husband misplaces his briefcase, you search for it. If you want to find a new house, you search for that, too. But in each case, the search involves using patterns of the familiar. These are things that if we have not searched specifically for them, we have searched for things like them. This search for "like-things" has provided contexts in our minds to use and aid us in our search for these identifiable things. This is also the case in business. If you want to hire a new secretary, you search for him or her. If you want to start a new business, you search for new ideas about the nature of that business. Again, these are all patterns of the familiar. And ultimately, if we do them enough times, they not only become patterns of the familiar, they become habits of thinking.

The search for originality is completely different. We have no earthly idea what the "thing" is that we are searching for. We have discussed six examples of searches for originality: Sony's search for a purpose, Jobs's search for knowledge, Dr. Nash's search for an original idea, 3M's search for a product, Miles Davis's search for musical expressions, and Prince Edvard's search for "self." And the common denominator was the same in each instance: they had no idea what they were searching for; thus, they had to rely on their instincts and improvise to find "it." Since we don't know what we're looking for, our Seeking Systems goad us into looking for it anyway, and our skills of observation help us collect meaning along the way. Because as Jobs said: "We can only connect the dots looking backwards. So you have to trust that the dots will somehow connect in [the] future."

It's easy to connect the dots with patterns of the familiar. You already know what most of the dots are. But the creation of "you;" the creation of the new "*Kind of Blue*;" the creation of the new "Snow White," the creation of the new "Apple;" these are all unique forms that defy patterns of the familiar. These new forms, as Plato defined them, cannot be attained by reason or reasoning. Because, as Plato explained, reasoning is reliant on likeness and likeness requires patterns of the familiar.

Einstein's work would have been a heck of a lot easier if the theory of relativity were a pattern of the familiar. Pasteur's work would also have been easier if vaccination were a pattern of the familiar. The beginning of *A Beautiful Mind* would have been a lot less interesting if Game Theory were a pattern of the familiar. They are not. In fact, they are analogies of the dissimilar or what Koestler refers to as bisociations. It is the ability to bring together two uncommon analogies that distinguishes insights that lead to breakthroughs from "incremental ideas" that improve patterns of the familiar.

Bisociation is the mental framework within which analogies of the dissimilar are connected to create insights. The chart on the opposite page provides several examples. We talked earlier about Archimedes' eureka moment when he connected the analogy of water and baths with the analogy of measurement of volume to determine the weight of Heiron's crown.

Jobs gave us an example of bisociation in his commencement speech when he linked calligraphy to the computer. As he said, the result was the wonderful typefaces they produced. Typefaces that, particularly for the creative industry, as well as the rest of us, proved indispensable. Through seeking, observing, collecting meaning, and personal significance, we prepare ourselves to make these connections.

So, how do we make these connections if we don't know what we're searching for? Seeking, observing, and collecting meanings helps prepare us to "know" the answer when we see it, and asking "different" questions helps us break the codes that bind us to patterns of the familiar and analogies of the similar.

Knowing the answer when we see it is called "ripeness." It is a preparedness of the mind to be able to make the connection and see the analogy when others can't or won't. The key reason you see the analogy and others don't is "personal significance," our lynchpin to appraisal. It is the single factor that determines what has meaning to you, and you alone.

Dissimilar Analogies and Their Resulting Insights		
1st Analogy	2nd Analogy	Breakthrough
Bath water	Measurement of Volume	Principle of Buoyancy
Music	Electricity	Telephone
Gospel Music	Medieval Music	Kind of Blue
Calligraphy	Computers	Typefaces
Portability	Tape Recorder	Sony Walkman
Surfing	Skating	Skateboarding
Ice skating	Wheels	Rollerblades/ In-line Skates
Immediacy	Picture-taking	Polaroid camera
Bicycle	Rooms w/ windows	Ferris Wheel
Sun	Rocks	Sundials
Sense of Touch	Reading	Braille
Contagious Viruses	Revolutions	*Tipping Point*
Entertainment	Downloading	iPod and iTunes Music Store
Book pages	Computer links	World Wide Web

A few years ago while working as a consultant at PricewaterhouseCoopers I happened to be sent to Chicago, my hometown, on a project. At the time, I was based in London and leading a team with nationals from several European countries. On this particular project, two consultants, one from The Netherlands and one from Germany, had made the trip with me. It was a long week. We had traveled from Europe to California interviewed companies there and then flew to Chicago for more interviews. Feeling exhausted after a long week, I suggested that we go to the beer garden at Navy Pier to relax.

It was a nice day. The sky was clear and visibility was perfect. Given the weather conditions, I suggested that we go to the Ninety-fifth floor of the John Hancock building to watch the sunset and see the magnificent views of the city. We all agreed and started planning at what time we should leave the beer garden to make it to the John Hancock before the sun went down. I looked at my watch and said we should leave in 45 minutes. One of the consultants, Frank, looked at the sun and said we should leave in 30 minutes. Which of us do you think was correct? It was Frank. By looking at the position of the sun Frank knew exactly when the sun was going to set. Why? Frank is German, and he had completed military service as required before attending university. In the military, being able to read the position of the sun is a survival skill.

Though we now rely on watches, as I did, our earliest ancestors were able to use the position of the sun to do exactly what Frank did; tell the time to survive. The sun had deep personal significance to our earliest ancestors. They studied it and the planets intensely. And, they couldn't survive or progress without it. Studying the sun enabled understanding the day, the month, the season, the migratory patterns of animals, and other events in nature. Not knowing the meaning of these observations meant starvation. Thus, the minds of our earliest ancestors were "ripe" to make the connection between two unrelated things: the sun in the sky and rocks on the ground. Just like every other insight that we've discussed, it was bisociation of the sun and rocks, using the shadows on the ground they cast, that created sundials and, moving on from sundials, calendars.

There's a final point to be raised here. Everyone has the skills necessary to create insight. To me, Dr. Lazarus's insight was correct; the most important thing is personal significance. So as we consider how highly standardized our work and personal lives are becoming for the benefit of productivity; it should give us pause. Standardization and mechanization take away seeking, collecting meaning, and emotion. Without those three things something really important is being lost—our ability to derive personal significance. Yet without this, it's difficult to ask the seemingly "stupid" questions that the code doesn't. To break the code, those questions must be asked.

The bisociations identified on page 191 resulted from creating uncommon links where others hadn't seen one previously. But to get their own minds around the possibility that these two unrelated things could be related, the inventor had to break with traditional thinking. Koestler refers to the habit of thinking in ways the world finds acceptable as codes. Further, he defines the frames of references that we infer by linking those codes together to form patterns of the familiar as matrices. When codes and matrices are used to form solutions or ideas, no new questions will arise because codes and matrices lead us to believe that we already know the answer. By abandoning the code, the historical matrix or frame of reference is no longer valid. Now, new questions can be raised that couldn't be considered previously. Apple's creation of iTunes Music Store is a good example of abandoning the code and forming a new matrix.

When Apple created iTunes Music Store most others in the technology and music industries were focused on the question, "How do we prevent illegal music downloads?" Apple saw the question differently, "How can we make entertainment accessible over the Internet legally?" Looking at the problem differently allowed Apple to associate entertainment with legal downloading. They effectively abandoned the codes that copyrights could not protect and that teens and young adults—key segments for the music industry—didn't want to pay for music acquired online. By not being bound to codes of the industry, they linked together iTunes with the iPod. And the rest, as they say, is history. Meanwhile, why the iPod has become a market revolution is clearly explained by Gladwell in the *Tipping Point*.

On the next page is a sample of the new questions that could have been raised as inventors broke the code to form a new matrix and create their insight.

Albert Einstein, for example, could never have come to the *Theory of Relativity* without breaking the code. Einstein struggled with the issue of time for several years. According to Perkins, Einstein said: "The fundamental issues had been brewing in [my] mind for some time. But one morning, in the spring of 1905, upon waking up, [I] found it all coming together. It appears that the key step was to challenge a fundamental and

News Questions that Broke the Code	
Albert Einstein	What if time isn't constant?
Surfers	What if I could surf in the winter on the sidewalk?
Ice Skaters	What if I could skate outdoors in the summertime?
Land's Daughter	What if I could see my picture now?
Sony	What if people could hold tape recorders in their hand?
Sir Tim Berners-Lee	What if I could view digital information as if I were browsing a book?
George Ferris	What if a bicycle wheel could make rooms with windows circle the sky?
Miles Davis	What if I slowed down the tempo of jazz?
Malcolm Gladwell	What if contagious viruses are just like market revolutions?
Steve Jobs	What if we could create fonts digitally?

simple premise we all take for granted: the constancy of time." Einstein questioned whether time always moved at the same speed in all places. We had assumed, until he proved otherwise, that the answer was "yes." By breaking this code—our habit of thinking about time in a certain way—Einstein asked a different question to create a new matrix: time is not constant. Einstein said:

"The formulation of a problem is often more essential than its solution, which may be merely a matter of mathematical or experiential skill. To raise new questions, new possibilities, to regard old questions from a new angle, requires creative imagination and marks real advance in science."

It was Edwin Land's 3-year old daughter who asked, "Why she couldn't see her picture now?" Children have their own definition for immediacy, which does not square at all with the code adults have assigned it. And of course, where a parent is concerned, few things can rival a child's wish in personal significance. Consequently Land, given his background of creating filters capable of polarizing light, was ripe to see and capitalize on the connection between immediacy and picture-taking. Once again, the code was broken and a new matrix created: seeing pictures instantly. The breakthrough, of course, was the Polaroid camera.

Finally, the question I find most interesting on the list is George Ferris's. Ferris created the first Ferris wheel for the Columbian Exposition in 1893 to rival the Eiffel Tower, the centerpiece of the Paris Exhibition in 1889. The Lemelson-MIT website states:

"The Exhibition's planners wanted something original, daring, and unique. Inspired, Ferris sketched a huge, revolving 'observation wheel' on a scrap of paper. Ferris's wheel was modeled on a bicycle wheel: as spokes to maintain the wheel's shape and balance, it had heavy beams; the forks in which the axle was set were two steel girder pyramids. The wheel was 264-feet high and carried 36 elegantly outfitted passenger cars, each of which could fit 40 people sitting or 60 people standing. The wheel was spun by either of two 1,000-horsepower steam engines, and stopped by an oversized air brake. At its opening on June 21, 1893, the Ferris wheel became the irresistible centerpiece of the Exhibition."

Because Ferris, unfortunately, died in 1836, just three years after his magnificent success, we will never know the story of his inspiration. Still, we do know that steel—of which the wheel was formed—had personal significance in his life. As a civil engineer, he specialized in constructing steel frameworks for bridges and tunnels. If you are curious what the original Ferris wheel might have looked like, take a look at the home page for the London Eye. It gives you a sense of what Ferris achieved 100 years earlier. Perhaps the next time we're on a Ferris wheel, we will be inspired, as we take in their majestic views, to ask a different question.

Creating Competencies by Following Your Instincts

At 22, Richard Drew was an engineering school dropout who made a living playing the banjo for dance clubs while continuing to earn his mechanical engineering degree through correspondence school at night. In 1923, he wrote a letter to 3M for a job opening as a lab assistant working with Bill Vievering. His first responsibilities involved checking raw materials and running tests on sandpaper. Next, he was assigned to make "handspreads" of their new Wetordry waterproof sandpaper. Later, he would take the handspreads to auto-body shops for testing.

On one of his visits, Drew observed auto-body workers growing frustrated when they removed butcher paper they had taped to cars they were painting. The adhesive on the tape was strong and peeled off some of the paint when it was removed. Naturally, this annoyed the auto-body workers because touching up the damaged areas increased costs. Having observed all of this, it was obvious to Drew that the painters needed tape with a gentler adhesive. So, Drew went back to 3M to experiment.

Drew worked relentlessly to solve the problem. Weeks went by without a solution. Eventually, McKnight required him to abandon the project and return to his responsibilities on the Wetordry sandpaper. In a work-style, which 3M calls "bootlegging," Drew continued to work on the problem. Finally, after two years of effort, he came up with a 2-inch wide strip of paper tape that was coated on the back with a rubber-based adhesive. Not knowing how much adhesive should be applied, he only coated one-quarter of the tape along each edge but not the middle. When the auto-body shop foreman tested the tape, it fell off. Frustrated with the sample, the foreman exclaimed: "Take this tape back to those Scotch bosses of yours and tell them to put more adhesive on it!"

That was the beginning of Scotch tape, which, coincidentally, celebrates its 75th birthday this year. Five years later, in 1930, Drew created Scotch Cellulose tape. It was the first waterproof, see-through, pressure-sensitive tape. Though the tape was originally sold to industrial customers such a bakers, grocers, and meat packers, its use spread to the consumer during the Great Depression. Stretched for cash, consumers used the tape liberally to repair all types of household goods, including book pages, documents, ripped window shades, and even dilapidated currency. As it celebrates this historical milestone, its longevity serves as an excellent example of the ability to use instincts to create enduring competencies.

Still, Drew's influence in competency-building extended far beyond one-off inventions. It embodied the idea of invention itself. Within 3M's environment, experimenting to create new insights was totally acceptable and mistakes were simply a part of learning. In fact, Drew's insistence on finding a solution for the adhesive tape problem led to 3M implementing the "15-percent rule." Under this rule, technical employees were encouraged to devote up to 15-percent of their work hours to independent projects. "With the development of Scotch masking tape, McKnight saw what Drew could do by saying, 'Management, you're wrong. I'm right, and I'm going to prove it!' After that, McKnight supported the idea that technical people could disagree with management, experiment, and do some fooling around on their own."

> "The 15 percent rule is unique to 3M. Most of the inventions that 3M depends on today came out of that kind of individual initiative ... You don't make a difference by just following orders."

McKnight's sensitivity to the need for inventive freedom also led to creating Products Fabrication Laboratory, known as the Pro-Fab Lab, led by Drew. At 35, Drew was successful but unhappy. 3M's organization had become more structured and organized. While their inventive spirit still prevailed, their approach to research and new product development was more methodical and formalized than suited Drew's free-wheeling, maverick style. The Pro-Fab Lab gave Drew the autonomy to create in a manner that best suited him and others like him.

During its 20-year lifetime, the lab was known for product breakthroughs that included Scotchlite reflective sheeting, Micropore surgical tape, foam tape, facemasks, and respirators. They also led experiments that—four decades later—enabled the development of the blockbuster product, Post-it-notes. Lew Lehr retired 3M chairman of the board and CEO said of Drew:

> "Dick Drew had an instinct that compelled him to push beyond reasonable limits and ... in some cases unreasonable limits. He was an irresistible force drawn toward any immovable object. "

McKnight's philosophy of people development and business building was decades ahead of his time. In *A Century of Innovation*, we were given some insight into his thinking:

> "McKnight saw business and the workplace differently. He understood interdependence as well as the importance of personal freedom. On his 60th anniversary with 3M he said: 'The best and hardest work is done in the spirit of adventure and challenge ... Mistakes will be made. But ... the mistakes he or she makes are not as serious

in the long run as the mistakes management will make if it is dictatorial and undertakes to tell those under its authority exactly how they must do their job. Management that is destructively critical when mistakes are made kills initiative, and it's essential that we have many people with initiative if we are to continue to grow.'

For a man who liked to control most aspects of his life, McKnight demonstrated a rare ability to see beyond his own needs. Delegating responsibility and authority, he said, 'requires considerable tolerance because good people ... are going to want to do their jobs in their own way.'

Born in a sod-covered house in South Dakota and raised working on his father's farm, where and how did McKnight develop these progressive ideas? McKnight's Scottish parents were pioneering settlers on the Midwestern prairie. From Joseph and Cordelia McKnight, the boy learned about risk-taking, self-determination and personal ambition. Growing up in an era when farmers were plagued by drought and grasshoppers, he learned about interdependence. Watching his father struggle to sustain and build the family farm from season to season taught McKnight the rudiments of entrepreneurship. Cordelia McKnight's faith in the goodness of people gave her son an enduring idealism. Joseph McKnight's activism on behalf of struggling fellow farmers taught his son to stand for his ideals.

When William broke the news to his parents that he would not be a farmer, one parent said to the other: "Let him have his dreams." From that simple response, McKnight learned how the support of personal freedom can set creativity free."

Clearly McKnight's parents also understood that innovating is a system and, as such, one must respond to our continuous need to change. As this chapter can easily become a book, I'm going to stop here. But I'd like to leave you with a final reflection from Paul E. Hansen, retired technical director, Nonwoven Technical Center. He spent many years working with Drew and later said everything he learned about working successfully in the lab, he learned from him. Of the many lessons he learned, this one seems especially relevant as we close this chapter. "Follow your instincts. Your instincts are actually your total experience in practice."

In the next chapter, we discuss the prime inhibitor of our instincts: fear. To be able to act on our instincts we need courage. As you have seen, to create new forms which reject patterns of the familiar we must be able to trust our belief systems that tell us this is true—follow it. Without courage, we follow our fears. As a result, our strategies for survival become not strategies of purpose, but strategies of fear. Let's learn how.

CHAPTER 8

Fear: The Challenge For All Times

Strategies Born of Fear

Jimmy Smith Jr. (aka Rabbit) is a rapper; at least, he'd like to be. Rap, as an art form, "is impromptu and fast-paced, topical and insightful, requiring skills of language, nuance, and keen observation, as well as emotional truth." For people like Rabbit, it was also a way to escape 8 Mile. "The psychological dividing line that separates him from where he wants to be and who he wants to be." He has the skills he needs, but there is something holding him back. That something is fear.

Rabbit's fear is that he will never get out of his reality. And like most of us, he spends all of his time honing his skills rather than dealing with his fear. So in his private world of "The Shelter's" bathroom, or when he's not in head-to-head competition, he's brilliant. The problem is: all animals are innately predisposed to sense fear, including humans.

Great rappers at "The Shelter" handily exploited strategies of fear. Why? They were fearless. Accepting their own weakness, they turned this into a strength. Strategies of fear focus on intimidation to get at the core of another's emotion. If they can get to the raw emotion of their opponent, they then attack their lack of focus. This loss of concentration interrupts the rapper's critical skill, insight, which is the key to clever, quick-witted comebacks. That's because rapping, like humor, relies on the ability of the rapper to make quick connections between seemingly unrelated things— using bisociation. If a rapper can invoke fear in his opponent, exposing that raw emotion diminishes his concentration. Rabbit was doomed before he even walked on the stage.

Rabbit's moment of insight into fear comes when his friend Cheddar Bob asks one of his seemingly "stupid" questions. Inspired, Rabbit not only exposes himself for what he is or what people perceive him to be, but he also exposes the other rapper for what he really is: unauthentic, with no street credibility.

In the Academy Award-winning song "*Lose Yourself,*" the rapper Eminem, who plays Rabbit in 8 Mile, asked a question: "If you had one shot, would you take it or just let it slide?" Interestingly, if we asked that question of corporate America, many would just let it slide. In my own research and others, it has been frequently observed that organizations engage excessively in risk avoiding behaviors. These behaviors, in spite of what the business's ideology may state, are being driven deep into the fabric of the organization and individuals to detrimental results. Why? The answer is simple, fear.

In this chapter, we examine how our strategies reflect our deepest fears. As we explore how fear and fear conditioning motivate us and guide our behavior, we learn that our strategies for success may in fact be merely smoke screens that attempt to mask our weaknesses. Let's start by understanding fear and fear conditioning.

Fear and Fear Conditioning

Joseph LeDoux is a foremost authority on the subject of fear and fear conditioning. He is the Henry and Lucy Moses Professor of Science in the Center for Neural Science at New York University. This section draws heavily on his work; however, the details of his research and theories on our emotional existence and development of self are chronicled in two excellent books: *Emotional Brain* and *Synaptic Self.* It is, therefore, impossible for me to summarize in great detail the inter-workings of his theories. Thus, I will explain the ideas of fear and fear conditioning from a very layperson perspective. I would urge you to do some seeking and discover for yourself how this cutting-edge research is helping us understand the realities of human existence.

How LeDoux came to help us understand fear and its underlying emotions further illustrates the principles discussed in the previous chapter. Quite simply, he followed his instincts and asked different questions. Twenty-five years ago when LeDoux was searching for a research focus, the hot new field was cognitive science—without emotion as we discussed in Chapter 3. But emotions were exactly what LeDoux was interested in. "In fact," says LeDoux, "my first grant on this topic in the early 1980s was turned down, because scientists reviewing my application believed it was impossible to scientifically study emotions." He did it anyway.

Fear conditioning has recently gained a great deal of prominence in everyday literature, due to the trauma of September 11th, other terrorist events, and recent natural disasters, such as Hurricane Katrina.

Fear is the most primitive of all human emotions. In Latin, there were three words that denoted fear: *timeo*, *metuo*, and *vereor*. While in Old English, there was only one word: danger. The emotion, fear, is a signal to the brain of potential danger that could threaten survival or inflict unwanted pain. The brain system has evolved in animals to help unconsciously discriminate potentially threatening objects in our environment and invoke strategies to avoid or defend against them.

We have all had a fearful event occur at some point during our lives. When such an event occurs, our bodies react in very predictable ways. Instantaneously, the body freezes, while neuro-chemicals flood into the brain that sharpens perception and singularly forces concentration on survival options. In conjunction with these neuro-chemical transmissions, blood flow is diverted to the major muscles to aid the possibility of flight or, if necessary, fight. The fear response system is automatic in most living species.

But within humans, our capacity to fear has grown beyond our basic need for immediate survival or to avoid pain. Our ability to project and imagine has allowed us to create beliefs about potentially fearful events that impact almost everything we do from crossing the street to catching an airplane. The reason for this is simple; we can be conditioned to fear. People's unwillingness to fly on airplanes post-September 11th or visit London following the transport system bombings are specific examples of fear conditioning. In fact, the website "wearenotafraid. com" was created in defiance to the terrorists, who through their actions attempt to condition fear.

Why we can be conditioned to fear is obvious; it enables survival. As LeDoux notes in the *Emotional Brain*:

> "Fear conditioning opens up channels of evolutionarily shaped responsivity to new environmental events, allowing novel stimuli that predict danger ... to gain control over tried-and-true ways of responding to danger. The danger predicted by these *learned trigger stimuli* can be real or imagined, concrete or abstract, allowing a great range of external (environmental) and internal (mental) conditions to serve as [conditioned stimuli]."

In other words, our fear system was created to protect us. What we haven't realized is that our fear systems weren't created to make us weaker they are there to make us stronger. It is yet another example of why we must move beyond habits of thinking to draw new conclusions and interpretations of what things mean. When we become locked into the habit of thinking a fear is something to be avoided and painful, each occurrence will be just that. Ultimately, these habits of thinking will become beliefs resistant to change because our subconscious actions reinforce them. Built inside of us is a process that, when we genuinely need it, will not only set off alarms but take control and drive movement. That is what emotion means in Latin, "to move." Fear is an emotion. Where we go wrong is believing we have to take control of a natural process: we can't control the process, we have to trust it. By trusting the process, our instincts will let us know if ever we are truly in danger when our emotional signals rise up to the level of feeling and create conscious awareness that we need to do something. By trying to hijack this process through controlling the experiences we are exposed to, we force ourselves into accepting primal responses to stimuli when they occur. Those responses have been coded into us through evolution and are counter to the myriad of possible responses available to us when we use our emotion in conjunction with our higher level–cognitive functions.

What LeDoux found through his work is that there are two paths our fear responses can take when faced with a threat stimulus. One he calls the high road, and one he calls the low road. His conception of this fear response path is provided below.

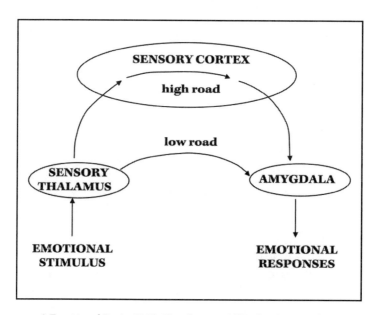

On the low road, the emotion signals go directly to the amygdala to force the fear response signal into action. This path is appropriate, for example, if you unintentionally walk out into traffic because you were in deep thought, or your child falls from a swing, or an animal dashes in front of your car, or if a suspicious person were to accost you in a parking lot. Our primal fear system would kick in, and you would be prepared to respond. Let's imagine for a moment that this suspicious person is indeed dangerous and forces you into the trunk of his car. Now, your fear system, if you don't panic, will allow you to begin to think through strategies for survival, like kicking out the car taillight, banging on the trunk, kicking in the back seat so that you can break the car window. If we trust the process of our fear system, it will help us use our higher cognitive functions, along the high road, to survive situations where death is not imminent.

As I write this, I am reminded of the woman here in Illinois whose car was literally sandwiched between two trucks. The car was flattened like a pancake. When the rescue crews arrived on the scene, they didn't even realize there was a car between the trucks. Yet, she survived. Why? She let her fear system direct her to a possible survival strategy. Realizing the trucks would collide, she scrunched as far down as she possibility could under the car's dashboard area. The trucks, being higher than the car, missed her head and body allowing her to survive. Trust your fear system's ability to help you survive and not only avoid pain but learn to deal with it.

Trying to consciously take control of or ignore our fear system gets us into a lot of trouble. Here are two examples.

Strategies of Fear

Rabbit's story in *8 Mile* illustrates the use of strategy at an individual level to mask fears. Organizations also attempt to hide their fears through strategies. Fear arises through fear conditioning. And when they interact subconsciously with beliefs and expectations, the resulting actions occur using the low road rather than the high road. Using the low road, the positive aspects of fear, such as its motivational underpinnings, occur without the benefit of knowledge-based processing that takes place on the high road and enables interface with the hippocampus convergence zone. The autonomous strategies that result on the low road often get us into more trouble than they're worth.

Wall Street and the reactions of investors condition public companies to fear. Notable exceptions to this are Google and Amazon who have publicly stated that they are building their companies for the long-term and will not allow their strategies to be dictated by the short-term desires of investors. Wall Street fuels the fear of uncertainty through their need for consistency in performance. This consistency is required to validate the valuations underlying stock prices. When the performance of the company is volatile, so is the underlying stock price. To uphold the expectations of the market analysts who predict the earnings performance and valuation of the stock, companies strive mightily to ensure that there are no surprises. To get this consistency, risk avoidance behaviors and strategies of fear emerge. A prominent fear amongst public companies is loss of market share. We have already seen the effects of this fear in the merger strategy of HP and Compaq. Still a more prominent example of this fear is Microsoft's historic battle with Netscape.

The Browser Wars, as they are known, are providing great lessons in strategy and strategy-making that will become classic case studies for many years to come. It is "wars," rather than war, because while the Netscape/Microsoft battle has ended, the Microsoft/ Mozilla war has just begun.

Remember the story about the submarine crew in Chapter 7? Well, that is exactly what happened to Microsoft. By the early 1990s, Microsoft had come to dominate the software market. They were, and still are, the largest software company in the world. While Microsoft was submerged under water—not even lifting the periscope—busily planning the release of Windows 95, the tool that would change the rules of competition and pace of technology as we knew it, was being created: the browser.

Sir Tim Berners-Lee, who was mentioned in the list of inventors on page 193, created the first rudimentary browser, which was "WorldWideWeb," in 1991. CERN, the European Organization for Nuclear Research in Geneva Switzerland, released the WorldWideWeb for general use. Though most people think the web and Internet are the same; actually, they are not. The Internet is a network of networks that enable packets of data to be sent around to other computers in the network. Sir Tim's insight was an application that allowed viewing of information on the Internet through the use of hypertext; hyperlinks; a method of connecting and transmitting data—Transmission Control Protocol; and a way to name servers on the network—Domain Name Servers. Two years later, a web browser called Mosaic, authored by Marc Andreessen and Eric Bana at the National Center for Supercomputing Applications (NCSA), was also released to the general public and began a revolution that ushered in new thinking about how business in the world could work.

Now before I admonish Microsoft, I'd like to make it clear that controlling market share of the browser market was definitely worth fighting for. But as my mother always told me, "It's not what you do; it's how you do it." Microsoft's problems stemmed not from winning, but from how they went about it. So, here's what happened.

In the winter of 1993, Andreessen graduated from the University of Illinois and took a position with a small firm in Silicon Valley. Jim Clark who was a legend in the Valley had recently left Silicon Graphics and was searching for a new opportunity. He contacted Andreessen to discuss possibilities for a new venture. They created Netscape (after a name change) to build and sell a web browser and servers. From its inception the company earned a profit, unlike most Internet start-ups. In its first full year of operation, the company earned $80 million in revenue and, at IPO, was valued at $7 billion.

Four months after Netscape's historic IPO on August 9, 1995, Microsoft responded. On Pearl Harbor Day in 1995, Bill Gates sent an e-mail to the troops at Microsoft indicating "a sleeping giant had been awakened from its slumber." Internet Explorer 1.0 ("IE") had been released as part of a Microsoft Windows 95 Plus Pack that August and IE 2.0 was released three months later in November. These versions of IE were mostly based on Mosaic software code that had been licensed from a company called Spyglass. However, Microsoft began to get serious with its browser technology with the release of IE 3.0, which was a major upgrade that still relied heavily on the Mosaic code. With the release of IE 4.0, Microsoft fully understood what it wanted to do with its browser technology and was no longer dependent on Spyglass. According to the Wikipedia's Browser Wars entry: "In October 1997, IE 4.0 was released. The release party in San Francisco featured a ten-foot tall letter "e" logo. Netscape employees showing up for work the following morning found that giant logo on their front lawn, with a sign attached which read 'From the IE team.'"

One of the first steps Microsoft took in its drive for market share was to backstab Spyglass and intimidate their customers. According to Eric W. Sink, who wrote the article *Memoirs from the Browser Wars*, "We got a loud wake up call when [Spyglass] tried to schedule [a] second conference for OEM browser customers. Our customers told us they weren't coming because Microsoft was beating them up."

When Microsoft decided to go for the browser market, they and Netscape engaged in what authors Michael Cusumano and David Yoffie of *Competing on Internet Time* called "judo strategy." In judo, the size of the opponent is used to its disadvantage making swiftness, flexibility, and leverage more important. Although Microsoft had become large and powerful, it had not forgotten how to be fleet-footed. When Microsoft engaged in judo strategy, it used fear in smart, motivational ways. For example, Microsoft had launched Microsoft Network (MSN) only months before Gates sent his Pearl Harbor Day e-mail. Yet, in its desire to embrace and extend the Internet, MSN's technology chief, Anthony Bay, and his core group was reassigned to the Internet software organization. Further, AOL and other online services, competitors to MSN, were offered placement of their icons on the Windows desktop—very valuable real estate. These deals meant Microsoft effectively abandoned MSN for the Internet. This strategy: swift, decisive, and thoughtful; dealt one of many deathblows to Netscape.

But when the competitors engaged in what the authors called "sumo strategy," Microsoft's primal fear response reared its ugly head. The primal fear response Microsoft used was intimidation of its customers and partners.

> "An internal 1996 Microsoft memo proposed a concentrated, no-holds-barred attack on Netscape. It directed managers to achieve 'exclusive licensing of Internet Explorer' at the five largest Internet service providers. The plan called for Microsoft negotiators to 'break most of Netscape's licensing deals. ... It pointed out that Microsoft could squeeze Netscape in the corporate world by exploiting Microsoft Windows licenses. ... 'The sales force must make it clear that it does not make any sense to buy Netscape Navigator.'"

This primal "no-holds-barred" fear response paved

the way for the anti-trust lawsuit that consumed the company for years, caused them to lose focus, and tarnished their brand in the eyes of consumers. The company is still fighting competition battles in the European Union ("EU") over their market tactics, only now they have to defend their actions regarding their MP3 video player strategy to the EU Commission as well.

In *Trust on Trial*, Richard McKenzie sums up the embarrassment Microsoft endured in the first phase of their trial:

> "Few legal observers were willing to give Microsoft an even chance of winning this first court battle. Jake Kirchner, a columnist for *PC Magazine*, summed up Microsoft's court position during the spring 1999 trial recess. "Microsoft and its executives have been thoroughly humiliated in the process. The government has ripped apart the testimony of just about every Microsoft witness, frequently using their own subpoenaed e-mails to contradict their prepared materials and in-court statements." He goes on to suggest that the Justice Department's lawyers have done an admirable job of making the Microsoft corporate hierarchy look like incompetent con artists at best—and liars and thieves at worst."

It's not what you do; it's how you do it. I believe Microsoft's actions were a direct result of fear, rather than the fearlessness they had become respected for. To engage in judo strategy, Microsoft had to think on its feet and come up with novel ways to win. Judo strategy took them back to a time when they were a scrappy start-up themselves. That was a time when they were fearless and used challenges as motivators, not inhibitors. When Microsoft engaged in sumo strategy, it used the primal fear code learned from corporate America. In corporate America, big companies use their power to intimidate. As Microsoft was growing up, and learning to deal with the "big boys" in Corporate America, they also learned to use the big boys' primal fear response to get through tough negotiations. Bill Gates made a mistake initially ignoring the potential of the Internet. Unfortunately, in his eagerness to correct that mistake, he let his fear instincts get the best of him.

If Gates had stepped back and trusted the process that made Microsoft the successful company that it is, their instincts to win would have helped them defeat Netscape. At the same time, they could have avoided the wraft of the US Government, consumers, and their partners by using the motivating component of fear. Yes, hindsight is 20/20. But in this case, a little trust on Microsoft's part would have gone a long way.

How do I know? The next story is about my own inability to trust the process of fear.

If the hypothesis of *Born to Win* is correct, it seems I was born to win. I had supportive parents, ample encouragement, and people expected great things from me. And as Robert Sternberg said, I gave them what they expected. Using their and my own expectations, I enacted an environment of success, even against the odds.

We grew up in a lower middle class neighborhood on the west side of Chicago. My father was a mechanic, and my mom was a factory inspector. We were happy, at least, I was. And I felt that I had everything that I needed.

My mom, on the other hand, had a really tough life growing up. Grandma left home when she was very young. She probably didn't know much about the world or about life, and she paid a severe price for that lack of knowledge. At a young age, she became pregnant out of wedlock. And, although my mother had a father figure in her life at times, at other times there was none. They were very poor, and her mother was, well, not a great mother—at least to her. Once my mother overheard my grandmother say she didn't want her. My mother grew up feeling unloved and unwanted.

To be honest, I don't know anything about my father's childhood. He died when I was eleven years old, and his life, like his death, isn't really talked about or dealt with by my family.

The reason for that is simple. To deal with things like the meaning of life or death requires one to deal with one's emotions, to open them up and explore them to the fullest to understand and capture their meanings and to allow the feeling from those emotions to rise to the surface. If that were to ever happen in our house, I think there would be an eruption.

You see, emotions were not allowed in our house. The only emotion expressed was anger: my mother's anger. The anger that has swollen up inside of her and has been eating her alive her entire life.

My temperament is a NT. I believe it's the same as my father's. I also believe it's what has helped me succeed against the odds. NTs are Thinkers: we don't rely heavily on our emotions, and, believe me, I didn't. Throughout my life, my strong analytical skills have always carried the day for me. They had to, because my emotions were too ill-prepared to help me.

I am happy to have been born who and what I am. The irony of my life is that, for better or worse, I like me. Even though, what me is, is far from perfect.

Whatever skills and resources I had, I put them to use as best I could. They got me through college, and I became an engineer. They got me into graduate school, and I became a consultant. They got me an international posting to work in London for PricewaterhouseCoopers. And, they helped me achieve tremendous things as a consultant there, until the day that I had to come face-to-face with my unaddressed emotions.

When my dad died, my mind—with its emotions neatly tucked away—rationalized it. My father had cancer, and, in the early-70s, if you had cancer, you died. There wasn't much that doctors could do. Dad had stomach cancer. It was excruciatingly painful for him, and we watched every day as he withered slowly away. My mom had to take care of him and us. His hospital bed and everything he needed was brought to our home, which allowed her to be his nurse. My mom loved my dad. This I know for sure. I believe that was one of the few times in her life, she felt loved and wanted. On that May day, just after my birthday, I arrived home from school. As usual, I went into my dad's room to see him. He wasn't there. I knew then and there what had happened; he was gone forever. I also know that I had lost something really important, but, in my mind, he was better off. And, in my mind, I would be okay.

On the outside, everything in my world was fine. I went to school. Got good grades. Participated in sports and other activities. Basically, I went about growing up just like every other kid around me.

When I started high school, I began dating the boy next door. Well, in this case, it was the boy across the alleyway, but he fit the description of the boy next door. He was a good kid. He never got into trouble, parents liked him, he was good at sports, and very responsible. He was, you know, the boy next door.

His father had died also, and sometimes we would talk about how much we missed our fathers. We became very close, and I became very attached. The deeper I became immersed in that relationship, the more attached I became. That attachment lasted seven years. Unfortunately, I was the only one that was attached. He wanted to move ahead with his life and date other girls. I wanted us to be together for the rest of our lives.

On a winter break during my sophomore year of college, we went out to dinner to celebrate his birthday. After dinner, we went back to his mother's house. As we lay on his bed, and he began to undress me, suddenly, I became unresponsive. I could hear him speak to me, but I couldn't answer. I couldn't move. He became anxious. Not knowing what to do, he called my mom. She and my oldest brother rushed to get me, and I was taken to the hospital. For several days, I was in a coma-like state. I couldn't move or talk. I don't know whether I could even feel. As I lay in the hospital bed, my family and friends watched helplessly.

After a period of days, or weeks, I don't know which; I woke up out of the coma-like state. In my usual fashion, I left the hospital and went on with life, as if nothing had happened. I went back to university and back to my classes. In fact, rather than take a break that summer, I stayed at school and worked part-time and took as many summer classes as I could. Junior year was coming up and there was a lot of work to do.

In the fall of that year, I moved out of the dorms and into an apartment with two of my girlfriends. The events of the past seemed to be behind me. Or maybe, I just hoped that was case. Of course, that was purely wishful thinking and later in the semester, I began having seizures. Finally, it was official. I had an emotional breakdown. My body had finally said, "deal with your emotions or else."

Rather than return to school second semester, I stayed at home and took classes at a local university. I also began seeing a psychiatrist. That lasted for about a nanosecond. There is nothing less useful for an INTJ, who is an introverted thinker, than to have someone stare at them for an hour waiting for them to speak about something they have no desire to talk about. At the end of the semester, I declared myself cured and went back to school.

Maybe, rest was all I needed. I went back to school and had one of my best semesters ever academically. I applied for and received a cooperative education assignment that allowed me to get some real experience and make some money. Getting real experience also helped me get my first job. It was hard work, but I met everyone's expectations. I graduated university, got a good job, and began preparing myself to become the success everyone expected me to be, including me. I was doing a great job of enacting the world I wanted to create.

Building buildings is interesting and challenging work. There's lots of complexity, which my mind likes, and there is also the awareness that you are creating something that reflects the essence of the society in which we live. Both these features drew me to construction. Still, once I got there, it never felt like that was the place I was meant to be. Eventually, graduate school became the next logical step, and I applied for admission.

After finishing business school, I became a consultant. I liked the people, and I liked the work, it suited me. More importantly, I was good at it, which helped me get an international posting in London.

Upon arriving in London, I remember how excited I was. Everything was new and different. The group I worked in was much smaller than the group I worked with in Chicago. There were only six of us. One girl left shortly after I arrived, so really there were only five. The great thing about being in a small group was if you did something well people noticed. And American workaholic that I was, getting noticed wasn't terribly challenging for me. Also, Lucinda, the partner-in-charge, was especially hands-off, which suited my thinking and work style very well. Moreover as a youngish partner, she was full of ideas and not afraid to take risks. My freethinking and creative spirit blossomed under her hands-off approach, and, together, we grew the team significantly.

My secondment had been agreed for a two-year

period, and, when the time came for me to leave, Lucinda and I struck a deal that enticed me to stay. I would be given wider leadership responsibility for building a team. She would support me, which she did. Over time, the team and consulting service that I created and led became very successful. Having been promoted rapidly during my time in London, I had reached the point of candidacy for partnership. Lucinda told me that my name along with others would be submitted to the partners to start the process.

A week or so later, I received a call from Lucinda, asking where I was and when I would return to the office. I told her I was in Ireland and that I would be back in London the next day. We agreed to talk first thing in the morning in her office.

Lucinda and I had a very comfortable relationship. We would both laugh so loudly that you could hear us across the entire floor of the building. Laughing was something we both greatly enjoyed. Unfortunately, there would be no laughing on this particular day. As Lucinda started talking I could hear her words, but the overwhelming rush of feelings that rose to the level of consciousness drowned them out. The feelings were intense and painful, as if a spear or dagger had been thrust into me with all force. I remember telling Lucinda, "I resign effective immediately," and going to pack my things. Probably for the first time in my life, I cried uncontrollably. My head pounded as if I had banged it against the wall. It felt like I had been stripped of everything that had value to me, and I had no idea how to reclaim it.

Although no one at the firm wanted me to leave. I left. And as the days and years since have passed, I finally came to realize why I had to.

I left for my own survival and to, finally, become. The rejection was too much for my psyche to handle, and my body, for the sake of its wellbeing, was saying, "Get out now!" So I did. Although I didn't know it then, I left to face my fears.

My fears stemmed from either the loss of my father, the loss of my first boyfriend, both or neither. It could have come from being beaten up at the age of eight when I moved to a new school. Really, it doesn't matter what the precipitating event was. What matters is that these exceptionally emotional events left me feeling abandoned and rejected, and those feelings, buried in my subconscious, went unaddressed. My body obviously gave me the first signal when, basically, it shut down. I wasn't dealing with my emotions, and it couldn't deal with the fact that I wouldn't. I didn't know to trust the process because I didn't know there was a process. Because our family didn't deal with its emotions, and because I preferred to not rely on my emotions, I didn't understand the full range of emotions possible within myself or in others.

The further fear conditioning that took root when rejection by the partners occurred, finally, opened deep scars that were buried long ago. And the behavioral outcomes that would have resulted, if I had stayed and acted on strategies of fear, could have led to serious problems in my professional life. If I had not dealt with my emotions, fear of rejection and abandonment, they would have consumed my life, just as my mother's anger consumes hers. Thankfully, my body knew the right thing to do, and I finally found the courage to follow my instincts, just as Rabbit did.

Fearful responses result from the body's attempt to create strategies to avoid future pain. Because the subconscious response is automatic, it draws on whatever script is available on the low road. If earlier scripts responded fearfully, a fearful response is what you will get. Worse still, as in my case, if the emotion triggered by the fearful event never rises to the level of consciousness, we aren't really aware of what we feel. All we know is that we responded. Most likely the response was not very satisfying. As we already said: "The results speak for themselves."

In my life, those results came during situations of rejection. My strategy of fear was to be perfect, remove any reason for people to criticize, blame, or dislike. The problem with strategies of perfection is there is no such thing. More importantly, the way people interpret your actions is potentially damaging to the relationships and environments you are trying to create. People think you're arrogant. You seem hypercritical and insensitive. People can become demoralized trying to live up to a standard they feel is unrealistic. And you push yourself and others to limits that are not sustainable or healthy in the long run. Clearly, these are not the results one would want from a strategy of perfection. But that's what you get when low road strategies, driven by fear, are dominating your actions and clouding your judgment.

Worse still, it doesn't take away the fear. I can recall instances where a rebuff has caused me to freeze, just as any animal does when it goes into a fear state. At these times, I would lose concentration and become unresponsive. Fear of being rejected also led me to try to control things that are essentially out of my control, like boyfriends leaving, colleagues agreeing with an idea or approach, or people liking or disliking me. The irony of that behavior is you surely get rejected: the boyfriend will definitely leave you; the colleague will never agree with you; and the people who don't like you will dislike you all the more.

Yet, for me, the worst part of this fear had been the anger. I spent most of my life being a witness to anger that I did not understand: anger in my mother, in myself, and in my sisters and brothers. I am not sure how you build a family on anger. What I do know is that all of our relationships have suffered because of it—our relationships with others and between ourselves.

Before We Move On, Let's Consider This

Given the change in our market economy to *more,* not less, uncertainty, companies engaging in strategies of fear—including copying rather than innovating—open themselves up to competitive threats because repeated use of primal responses to fear becomes predictable. And due to the resistance of beliefs to change, these ingrained habits of the familiar hinder the success of new strategies when entrenched expectations deter desired behavioral changes in employees. The reason for this entrenched behavior is fear conditioning. Examples of potential fear conditioning include: a manager scolding a new recruit for an overly ambitious presentation; a supervisor demoralizing a line worker for not doing it his way; a boss saying "great idea, but we can't possibility achieve this." With repeated and punitive reinforcement, these acts condition employees to fear taking risks and/or limit their motivation. At its extreme, it institutionalizes a fear of innovation and rewards risk-avoidance. These fears are then reflected in the actions of employees and the results of the firm, which speak for themselves.

Until we learn to trust the process we cannot move these responses up to the high road where we can engage our full range of possible survival strategies that enable us to become. It's not always that we don't want to change, but the emotions underlying fear reside in an area of our brain that is resistant to change. Moreover, dealing with certain emotions means dredging up pain, and we instinctively work to avoid this, as we were biologically organized to do.

In the final chapter, we return to our discussion of the self to connect the five characteristics and start a new path to become.

Self: Becoming a Whole Person

Learning to Become A Whole Person

This chapters continues our discussion on the characteristic of purpose, self, which requires us to move from being a personality to a whole person.

The Self: Trusting the Process to Become

Without the self, there is no need for purpose. Creating self requires purpose, which drives our continual need to seek and refine meaning. In explaining the five characteristics of purpose, I struggled with whether the self comes first or last. Ultimately, I understood that it comes last because in our quest to become, this is not where we start. As we learn, grow, and evolve, we move from being a personality, to become, if we are lucky, a whole person, where we realize our self-identity. As a whole person, not only are we comfortable (not cocky) in our personality, we also have the ability to adeptly navigate the inherent weaknesses of our personality as well. Let's take a look again at Prince Edvard.

Like most of us, Edvard relied heavily on his temperament to carry him through life. He was strong-willed and independent. Yet, he was all too aware of his weaknesses, and he feared them. More importantly, the expectation that he was to live up to his father's legacy as a confident and compelling Ruler seemed overwhelming. As his father tells Edvard before they enter the meeting to discuss the National Strike: "One day, you will be the 51st Ruler of the longest continuous monarchy in the history of the world. It's a monarchy that still requires the participation of the King in the working sessions of the government. So, if I ask you whether you are prepared, it is not an insignificant question." But in Edvard's heart, as he confesses to Paige, he feels he is "young, scared, and not ready for the hard choices that he has to make. It's not easy having to deal with that kind of pressure." And, unfortunately, Prince Edvard's emotional building blocks seem to be damaged by his domineering and overbearing mother, who does not seem very warm, loving, compassionate, sensitive, or understanding. She has sacrificed herself to be who she had to become and feels that everyone else must do the same, including Paige and Edvard.

Due to the damage to his emotional building blocks, Prince Edvard engages in behaviors like promiscuity and recklessness. The issues that damaged his emotional building blocks have hindered his ability to use evolutionary codes that our psyche can draw on to help us navigate our type weaknesses and address conscious fears developed through conditioning. These evolutionary codes are called "archetypes."

Temperament mires us in patterns of the familiar and requires that we stick to the codes. The codes become familiar and create matrices because of the way we catalog sensory data to create meaning. Throughout our development of self, as we work to refine our temperament, archetypes lie in wait, ready to be awakened when we need them. During the formidable years of youth, love, security, trust in authority figures, intimacy, humility, responsibility, instincts, and other emotional building blocks are required to support self-development and the ability to address the inevitable hardships of emotional life: rejection, abandonment or loss, exploitation, shyness, uncertainty, deceit, boredom, and others. Without appropriate emotional building blocks, the subconscious struggles to deal with reactions to these emotional upheavals for which it has no patterns of habit to rely on. When those building blocks are not properly formed, our fear system defaults to the low road where our primal fear responses reside. Those primal fear responses create shadow behaviors that have also been coded into use through evolution. Edvard's shadow behaviors were promiscuity and recklessness. My shadow behavior was perfection.

Archetypes awaken when a type weakness needs help to successfully manage a difficult situation. In Edvard's case for example, the competencies he had developed through his type were literature and mechanics. But his type weaknesses left him feeling unsure about his abilities in diplomacy and political negotiations, skills he needed for working with the government.

After returning to Denmark, his type weakness is tested when the strike deadline approaches and an agreement must be reached to avoid the national strike. As the meeting gets heated, Edvard reacts on instinct. He begins to think about how he felt as a poor college student working for a tiny wage. In telling the story, he recalls something Paige's father had told him about interdependence. Thinking about how that applied to the negotiation stalemate, he realized there were three parties affected by the outcome of the settlement, but that only two parties were contributing to the trade-off. His insight was to draw in all three parties to give and take so that an agreement could be reached. By trusting his instinct, Edvard was able to create an insight about a problem for which type skills were less refined. The instinct he awoke was an archetype.

What scientists are beginning to confirm about man is that certain behavioral characteristics have been coded into us through evolution. We just discussed one, our fear system. The reaction to freeze momentarily has been coded into most animals through evolution. Another that we mentioned briefly in chapter 5 is facial expression. Paul Ekman studied facial expressions in detail. In his book, *Emotions Revealed*, he explains how facial expressions help us understand people's underlying emotions even when they don't openly reveal them. As the saying goes, "It shows on your face." Well through his work, Ekman has demonstrated that facial expressions are universal. Meaning a smile is a smile no matter where you are in the world. When you travel to remote international locales you learn this firsthand. Few in the remote jungles of Thailand speak English. You communicate through body language and facial expression, and it works.

What Jung tried to explain in his writings, without the benefit of fear studies, facial expressions, or neurological explanations for how consciousness works (provided by Damasio), is our psyche has evolutionary codes as well. They have evolved with us over time, just as our fear system, facial expressions, and consciousness did. Facial expressions are outward manifestations of our emotions, so through a long and painstaking process of observation, Ekman was able to identify what the facial codes were for particular emotions. In *Blink*, Gladwell provides a detailed example of this. LeDoux could see the outward manifestation of the emotion fear, but he had to work through a surgical extraction process on rats to determine exactly how it worked. By doing so, he uncovered the evolutionary code of fear.

Our temperament represents outward manifestations of evolutionary codes for mental processing. Before neurology, we could not see these hidden codes of temperament or belief in the brain. Now we can at least identify when they occur by observing the brain light up using a PET scan and pairing the results with various kinds of cognitive tests. We mentioned one example of this in Chapter 2: Canli's work on the brains of introverts and extroverts. Damasio's work helped us understand the difference between emotions and feelings by explaining the nature of consciousness. He also presented an explanation for how intuition, an aspect of temperament, occurs in the brain. In the area of belief, recently a study indicated that the brains of racially biased individuals are emotionally drained after an encounter with an individual of a different race. These are just a few of many different studies underway to help us better understand the codes of temperament and belief.

Jung intuited that the presence of archetypes is potential, not kinetic, energy. Now, bear with me for a moment while the engineer in me attempts to explain this. I'm taking the strict view that there are only two forms of energy: potential and kinetic. Kinetic energy is energy in motion. Anytime we see something moving, that's kinetic energy. Potential energy is energy that is waiting for motion. It *can* move, but there has to be an impetus—driving force—to get it moving. If potential energy never gets this driving force, it lies dormant, unused. Our temperament works on kinetic energy. Our emotions make us aware of the things around us, and, through our feelings, urges rise to the level of consciousness. Goaded by our seeking drive, those urges prompt us to go out and explore the world. Our synapses that get the emotional signals are pre-wired to use the temperament codes first, making them kinetic. But that same seeking drive occasionally pushes us to explore things that make no sense to us because they seem counter to the codes of our temperament and the patterns of habit that we learned from observing our environment. Those instincts are the awakening of our potential energy: the energy waiting to be used. This potential energy, as described by Jung, represents the archetypes.

Archetypal behavior resides in all of us, waiting patiently to be used. Our instincts prompt us when it's necessary to rely on our archetype rather than our type. The reason archetypes exist seems obvious when we think about how mental processing works in opposites. Some functions and attitudes are dominant and others are weak. If we only had our temperament to rely on we would become very one-dimensional. We would have great difficulty seeing things from varying perspectives and understanding the worlds of others. The type with the most power and influence would come to dominate the environment to the detriment of all other types. Ultimately, this would create harmful imbalances in the world's environment. Plasticity of our synapses gives us the ability to extend our responses beyond those pre-coded by our type. However, the process of learning is, in some cases, necessarily slow, and lapses may occur where we default to our pre-coded behavior.

The archetypal component of self was evolution's "quick and dirty" answer to this problem. The pattern of behavior that would balance a type weakness was pre-coded so it wouldn't have to be learned just as our reactions to fear don't have to be learned. The behavior was meant to be instinctive: we only had to trust our self and use it. When we ignore the instinct, usually because of fear, our bodies still have to react, so it defaults to another evolutionary code: the primal fear code. When the primal fear code is invoked, a shadow behavior emerges from our primal emotional responses. They take the low road and are acted on without thought or reflection. They are automatic. It works, but, as we already discussed, the results are less than satisfactory. To unlearn these responses, plasticity helps us develop intelligent emotional responses that connect within our convergence zone, using the high road. Again, we must remember that learning takes time. We can also, through patterns of habit, allow an archetype to become dominant, which creates other problems.

Carol Pearson, in *Awakening the Heroes Within*, identified twelve archetypal behaviors that we have at our disposal for use when our type codes are insufficient to deal with an event within our environment. Below, I provide one example of the many shadow responses defaulted to when we don't follow our instincts that allow us to awaken the archetypal behaviors, as she identified them.

Archetypes, Fears, and Shadow Responses		
Archetype	Fear	Shadow Response
Innocent	Abandonment	Denial
Orphan	Exploitation	Blaming
Warrior	Weakness	Unethical Behavior
Caregiver	Selfishness	Manipulation
Seeker	Conformity	Perfectionism
Lover	Loss of love	Promiscuity
Destroyer	Death	Self Destruction
Creator	Unauthentic	Work-a-holism
Ruler	Uncertainty	Control Freak
Magician	Wickedness	Belittling
Sage	Deception	Dogmatism
Fool	Boredom	Distasteful Hedonism

© Awakening the Heroes Within, 1991, HarperCollins Publisher.

Awakening the Archetypes to Become

In case you haven't already guessed, what I should have worked to become is a writer. Throughout my youth that was obvious, in spite of my natural math and science ability. What I loved to do was read and write. Writing wasn't something I worked at; it was something I just did. I did it, because I loved it.

When I went to college, I went to study journalism. I chose the college that I did specifically because it was known for having a good journalism program. In our high school yearbook, it says that I was going to be an investigative reporter. And on the day that I graduated from high school, I was.

That fall, classes started, and I couldn't have been more excited. One of my best friends from high school was my roommate, and we had a great dorm room. She was majoring in journalism, too. We worked on the high school newspaper together. She, like Lucinda, laughed a lot. I think I'm totally drawn to people who like to laugh. Anyway, classes started, and I wanted to work in the school news studio. It had a TV news camera and an anchor desk—so to speak—and an opportunity to learn. I was very excited.

If you don't know much about Chicago, it's a very segregated city. I grew up on the west side in an African American community. The area where we lived borders a Mexican-American community. Until I became twelve years old, I went to an all-black school. At the time, it only housed students through the sixth grade. So, for seventh grade, I had to change schools. Given the location of our homes, everyone in our community had to transfer to the school in the Mexican-American community. It was the only one available in our district. Personally, I was very happy for the change because my new friends were now African American, Filipino, and Mexican-American. I loved my friends, especially, Valentine, who was Philippine. And, I had a special kinship with Alicia, who also wanted to be a writer. Those were especially happy times in my life. And I thrived in that environment.

After two years, we had to change schools once again for high school. The class I had been assigned to during my upper grades—7th and 8th—was termed "accelerated," meaning we were the students with the highest potential. We took special classes and were allowed to apply and take the entrance examinations for college preparatory schools. At that time, there were only two college preparatory schools in the city. A new college preparatory school would open my freshman year, but then, as it is now, admittance was highly political.

Each year, of course, we are given standardized tests. Our tests during the 8th year would be used to determine high school admission. For some reason, I had not taken the test that year.

In school, I was never the straight "A" student, but I had raw intellectual firepower, and it showed. I would be the kid who "out-of-the-blue" could solve the toughest math problem or write an award-winning essay. When the time came to put in high school applications, mine could not be sent because of the missing test scores. Of course, my teacher was fully aware that I had not taken the test, but did not schedule time for me to take it. It was only when my mother inquired why my name wasn't being submitted to one of the schools for their entrance process that the oversight was corrected.

Unfortunately, teachers are not unbiased in their actions, and mine was no exception. My homeroom teacher was very good friends with our social studies teacher who was responsible for administering our constitution exam required for graduation. To take the exam, we needed to purchase a booklet to study. Living in a poor area, everyone could not afford to purchase the book, which I thought was unfair. So, I petitioned the school against the teacher, and won. Unfortunately, that didn't make my homeroom teacher very happy, so she was not about to go out of her way to help me get into the high school of my choice.

At my mother's insistence, it was arranged for me to take the required exam. Even though I wasn't the straight A student—Mary Melendes was—my standardized test score was exceptional. Still, I didn't get to go to high school with my friends because my application was sent after the deadline. I went to one school, and all of my friends went to another.

Although I made many friends in high school who are still my friends to this day, a part of me felt I should have been somewhere else.

That day in the university newsroom, I can remember how excited I was. It was the first day on my path to becoming Christiane Amanpour. I couldn't wait. We were allowed to operate the camera, take turns sitting in the news chair, and explore our new environment. I wondered what it would be like to interview famous people. How would I learn all the stuff about the world I needed to know to ask really insightful questions? Did I have to wear make-up? " I don't really like make-up," I thought. I had a million questions about the future.

But as the event continued, my mood changed. I

went from excitement to doubt. I questioned whether I fit in. I questioned whether this was the right decision. And, I questioned the facial expressions of the other students in the studio with me. As I connect the dots backwards, what I saw in the faces of my fellow journalism students was the same thing I saw in the faces of the mean kids at my new school in third grade; it was the same thing I saw in the face of my eighth grade teacher and her friend after the petition; it was the same thing I saw in the face of the man at the canteen stand. I saw rejection. The thing I feared most.

That night, on the third day of university, I changed my major. I went through the college catalogue and tried to find something else that had interest to me. The only other thing that I could think of was engineering. I was good at math, and I like science, so I decided to change my major. The next morning, I went to the construction department in the school of engineering to see the dean. Although I didn't have an appointment, he agreed to meet with me anyway. I sat down in the chair at the front of his desk and told him that I wanted to transfer into the program. He looked at me, and once again, there was that expression. He explained, as nicely as he could, that he was sorry but in order to join the program I needed to have certain scores on my ACT exam. Timidly, I pulled my transcript out of the folder I was carrying and handed it to him. After a moment or two, I found my composure, and said, "But I have those scores."

My social studies teacher wrote the following in my eighth-grade memories book: "Being exceptional carries with it responsibility. The <u>real</u> exceptional individuals recognize this fact and live up to their possibilities." She's right. And when I stood up for those less fortunate in my class, I did just that. I invoked the warrior archetype to achieve change. Unfortunately, I did not always wisely respond to my archetypes. At varying developmental stages of my life, I suppressed five of the twelve archetypes: Innocence, Orphaning, Seeking, Loving, and Foolishness. Not trusting myself prevented me from becoming: not just a writer, but also a whole person. Many aspects of my relationships with the world were impaired by my inability to use and enjoy the full range of my emotions. Moreover, my primal fear responses, as I have already mentioned, prevented me from realizing the things I wanted most: love and professional achievement.

Like many other people on this planet, my emotional building blocks were seriously in need of more than just a little remedial work. They needed a complete upgrade!

Clearly, I am not alone. If we consider the numerous articles written about managers' unproductive behaviors, it's obvious that these issues spill over into the workplace. It really is time that we, as individuals, addressed them.

In *Built to Last*, Collins and Porras identified an odd behavioral pattern in the visionary companies. They referred to this behavior through the yin/yan symbol from Chinese philosophy. One example is "a fixed core ideology" and "vigorous change and movement." What these researchers identified was well-developed type/archetype behavior on the part of the company's leadership. The visionary companies realized their purpose. Not because the ideology was drummed into every employee's head, but because the leadership's actions supported well-developed type/archetype behavior that allowed employees to use the five characteristics effectively to become. These authors' efforts are to be applauded given that it was the first study to identify most of the behavioral characteristics companies need to engage to function as a whole organization rather than a character type, as defined in Bridges's *Character of the Organization* and other published documents on the subject. And, the futures of our children depend mightily on our ability to attain this balance once again.

Final Thoughts Before I Close

The biggest problem with our temperament, and our belief system supporting it, is its natural inclination to conveniently serve as a crutch. Because it allows us to conceive and act out our world as if it were certain, it also allows us to not adjust expectations, not trust our instincts, not work with others to support survival, or deal with the shadow responses created by our primal reactions to fear.

We all have expectations, but shutting out the real world—especially our fears—won't fulfill them. To achieve our goals, dreams, and desires, acting-out what we expect is a necessary aspect of creation. Still we have to listen to our instincts which tell us when our belief dimensions can no longer draw the distinction between "acting-out" and "blocking-out." Creation of real world environments that move beyond acting-out to become natural evolutions and extensions of our true selves requires us to be able to see through our delusions of absolute truth (that cause blocking-out) to re-engage relative truth, which constantly changes and necessitates us changing with it.

Essentially—if we let it—blocking out prevents us from doing what we are innately created to do: evolve. We can only do that by moving beyond our temperament and beliefs through change. As biological systems, like other systems, to change, we must respond. Our bodies send us the signals; it's our job to fearlessly act on them. When we do, we become a whole person as we learn to allow our type and the archetypes to work together in harmony.

When I spoke to Philip Wright, the Global Head of Corporate Finance in London, about my desire to leave PricewaterhouseCoopers, he said: "Franchee, it's not just that we want you to be a partner. We think you're a future star."

Yes, maybe, I can be a star; we all can. But only if we move beyond the delusional world that beliefs and temperament conveniently create for us, to have the courage to become. Jeff Bezos is right. We don't choose our passions; our passions choose us. Still, we have to have the courage to use them. Let go of your fears, use your instincts, go "act-out" your environment with others who share your dreams, and let your passion find you. Then, and, only then, can purpose begin its work.

If everything in my emotional life had worked, as evolution intended, I could never have written this book. It would have lacked the personal significance that allowed me to create meaning. But someone had to write it. I'm just thankful God chose me to do it.

Acknowledgements

Almost exactly four years ago, I woke up one morning that wasn't any different from any other morning. I turned to my then boyfriend, Benedikt, gave him a kiss good morning and went to prepare our breakfast. But, that morning was different, because that morning I decided I needed to follow my purpose, or at least try to find it. During breakfast, I told Benedikt that I planned to write a book. I'm sure he thought I was crazy, but I started the process anyway. Four years later, I've completed it. Although at times he began to believe that perhaps I really had gone insane, he supported me nonetheless. Benedikt, I have sincerely appreciated your love, support, and friendship.

I have received so much help and generosity from so many people that I'm not sure where to begin. As with most things, it's probably best to start at the top. I would like to thank my Mom for bearing with me during what has been a considerable period of uncertainty in my life. Additionally, I'd like to thank my brother Anthony Harmon for taking everything off my plate, so I could focus and get the book completed. Anthony, I love you so much sometimes it hurts. I would also like to thank my sister-in-law Linda Sagan for being a great person and a great sister. I'd like to thank my nieces and nephew, Bill and Laura Harrier and Crystal Harmon, for being a great source of distraction when I felt my head would explode from thinking too much. And Meg Sagan, thanks for being the first brave soul to read what ultimately became my manuscript.

A lot of people I have worked with over the years provided moral and practical support during this effort. At the top of this list is Gerry McCrory. During my time in London and Ireland, I learned a great deal about technology and innovation. Without Gerry's confidence in me, this would never have happened. Thank you Gerry. You have great instincts, and I hope you continue to follow them. I would also like to thank the senior management teams in Crucible's investment portfolio for sharing their time and their knowledge. I particularly want to thank Tom Higgins and Paul McBride of Interactive Enterprises. You presented me with great consulting challenges, and I thank you for trusting me to deliver. Anne Driscoll quickly went from being an executive recruiter to being a friend. Anne, I appreciate your constant support and friendship. This document has gone through many drafts, re-writes, and revisions. I'd like to thank Stephanie Woodson for being the first guinea pig who read and commented on very early drafts of my thinking. You always need people in your life who tell you like it is. For me, that's Adam Bergstein. Adam, I always appreciate your candor, your admiration, and your support. Thank you. Whenever I reached out to him no matter how busy he was Adam Gutstein has always been there for me. Adam, thank you for supporting and believing. It has meant a lot. At an Executive's Club presentation here in Chicago this past summer, I went up to Richard Notebaert after his keynote presentation and asked if his company would participate in the book. Without hesitation, he said, "yes." Thank you Mr. Notebaert and Jill Hollingsworth for your help. I'd like to thank the Executive Program of the University of Chicago Graduate School of Business for letting me interview their executive MBAs as part of my research. I'd also like to thank the XPers who participated in the focus group interview: Jenna Brown, Hernando Madronero, Paul Shekoski, Douglas Glade, and

Alejandro Videla. On a pro-bono basis, Digiserve in Ireland developed an on-line survey to capture the initial research data through the hard work of Fiachra O'Marcaigh and Daragh Mulvey. I am deeply indebted to Colm Grealy for his generosity in providing Digiserve resources to perform this work. I also appreciated the help of Anne Goodchild, who analyzed the research data for me. A great deal of effort went into searching for things that we didn't know what we were searching for, and I am indebted to Jayshree Patel for undertaking this initial search effort with me and to her husband Ash, who supported her efforts. To the many partners and former partners at PwC, particularly Lucinda Spicer, Philip D. Wright, Ian Coleman, Robert Conway, John Bromfield, Peter Spratt, Alistair Levack, Alistair MacWilson, John Harley, Tim Ogier, John Rugman, Maggie Mullen, and others, I'd like to say thank you for helping to develop my consulting skills to their fullest, without which this effort would have seemed insurmountable. Best wishes to all of you. And to the staff and former staff of PwC, particularly, the former members of the High-tech Toolkit team, thank you for giving me the opportunity to understand what leadership is all about and giving me the courage to work towards my true self.

Last, but by no means least, I'd like to thank Ania Kitka, who welcomed my niece Crystal and me into her life. You were there to give me a crash course in motherhood when I needed it. And, you have been there supporting me through some pretty difficult times. I am very lucky to have you as my friend. Thank you. Finally, to Gunnar Kauke, I'm not sure what to say. I don't know how you know what you know, but thank you for opening my eyes to what was really going on. Somehow, thank you seems pretty inadequate for all you've done.

Bibliography

BOOKS LISTED ALPHABETICALLY

A Century of Innovation, St. Paul, Minnesota, 3M Company, 2002.

Abell, Derek F., *Defining the Business: The Starting Point of Strategic Planning*, Englewood Cliffs, New Jersey, Prentice Hall, 1980.

Anastasi, Anne, *Psychological Testing*, New York, New York, Macmillian and Company, 1988.

Andrews, Kenneth, *The Concept of Corporate Strategy*, Homewood, IL, Irwin, 1987.

Ansoff, H.I., *Corporate Strategy*, New York, New York, McGraw-Hill, 1965.

Bernstein, Peter L., *Against the Gods: The Remarkable Story of Risk*, New York, New York, John Wiley & Sons, 1996.

Boudon, Raymond, *The Origin of Values,* New Brunswick, New Jersey, Transaction Publishers, 2001.

Bowman, E.H., *Strategy Changes,* New York, New York, Harper Business, 1990.

Branddenburger, Adam M, and Nalebuff, Barry J, *Co-opetition*, New York, New York, Currency Doubleday, 1996.

Branquinho, Joao, *The Foundations of Cognitive Science*, Oxford, England, Clarendon Press, 2001.

Bridges, William, *The Character of Organizations*, Palo Alto, California, Davis-Black Publishing, 2000.

Briggs-Meyers, Isabelle, and Meyers, Peter B, *Gifts Differing*, Palo Alto, California, Davis-Black Publishing, 1980.

Brody, Nathan, *Human Motivation: Commentary on Goal-Directed Action*, New York, New York, Academic Press, Inc., 1983.

Burgelman, Robert A., *Strategy is Destiny: How Strategy-making Shapes a Company's Future*, New York, New York, The Free Press, 2002.

Campbell, Andrew, and Summers-Luchs, Kathleen, *Core Competency-Based Strategy*, London, England, International Thomson Business Press, 1997.

Chandler, A.D. Jr, *Strategy and Structure: Chapters in the History of the Industrial Empire*, Cambridge, MA, MIT Press, 1962.

Childs, John L., *Amercian Pragmatism and Education*, New York, New York, Henry Holt and Company, 1956.

Christensen, C.R., and Andrews, K.R., and Bower, J.L., *Business Policy: Text and Cases*, Homewood, IL, Irwin, 1982.

Clampitt, Philip G., and DeKoch, Robert J., *Embracing Uncertainty*, Armonk, New York, M. E. Sharpe, Inc., 2001.

Cole, A.H., *Business Enterprise in Its Social Setting*, Cambridge, Massachusetts, Harvard University Press, 1959.

Collins, James C., and Porras, Jerry I., *Built to Last*, New York, New York, HarperBusiness Essentials, 2002.

Coutrney, Hugh, *20/20 Foresight*, Boston, Massachusetts, HBS Press, 2001.

Covey, Stephen R, *The Seven Habits of Highly Effective People*, Great Britain, Simon & Schuster, 1989.

Csikszentmihalyi, Mihaly, *The Evolving Self*, New York, New York, HarperCollins Publishers, Inc., 1994.

Cusumano, Michael A., and Yoffie, David B., *Competing on*

Internet Time, New York, New York, The Free Press, 1998.

Damasio, Antonio, *Descartes' Error*, New York, New York, Quill, 2000.

Damasio, Antonio, *Looking for Spinoza*, Orlando, Florida, Harcourt, Brace and Company, 2003.

Damasio, Antonio, *The Feeling of What Happens*, Orlando, Florida, Harcourt, Brace and Company, 1999.

Davis, Miles, and Troupe, Qunicy, *Miles: The Autobiography*, New York, New York, Simon & Schuster, 1989.

Deal, Terrence E., and Kennedy, Allan A., *Corporate Cultures*, Reading, Massachusetts, Addison-Wesley, 1982.

Deci, Edward L., and Ryan, Richard M., *Intrinsic Motivation and Self-Determination*, New York, New York, Plenum, 1985.

Dewey, John, *Democracy and Education*, New York, New York, The MacMillian Company, 1916.

Dewey, John, *Experience and Nature*, New York, New York, WW Norton & Company, 1929.

Dewey, John, *The Quest for Certainty: A Study of the Relation of Knowledge and Action*, New York, New York, Minton, Balch, 1929.

deWit, Bob, and Mayer, Ron, *Strategy*, London, England, International Thomson Business Press, 1998.

Dozier, Rush W., *Fear Itself*, New York, New York, St. Martin's Press, 1998.

Drucker, Peter F., *Management: Task, Responsibilities, Practices*, New York, New York, Harper & Row, Inc., 1985.

Drucker, Peter F., *The Concept of the Corporation*, New Brunswick, New Jersey, Transaction Publishers, 2001.

Dyert, R.M., and March, J.G., *A Behavioural Theory of the Firm*, Englewood Cliffs, New Jersey, Prentice Hall, 1963.

Eden, Colin, and Ackermann, Fran, *Making Strategy*, London, England, Sage Publications, 1998.

Eichenbaum, Howard, and Bodkin, J. Alexander, *Belief and Knowledge as Distinct Forms of Memory*, Cambridge, Massachusetts, Memory, Brain, and Belief, 2001.

Ekman, Paul, *Emotions Revealed*, New York, New York, Henry Holt and Company, 2004.

Ekman, Paul, and Davidson, Richard J., *The Nature of Emotion*, New York, New York, Oxford University Press, 1994.

Ellsworth, Richard R., *Leading with Purpose*, Stanford, California, Stanford Business Books, 2002.

Elster, Jon, *Alchemies of the Mind: Rationality and the Emotions*, Cambridge, United Kingdom, Cambridge University Press, 1999.

Eysenck, Hans Jurgen, *The Biological Basis of Personality*, Springfield, Illinois, Thomas, 1967.

Flood, Patrick, *Managing strategy Implementation: An Organizational Behaviour Perspective*, Oxford, England, Blackwell Publishers Ltd., 2000.

Florida, Richard, *The Rise of the Creative Class*, New York, New York, Basic Books, 2002.

Fodor, Jerry A., *The Language of Thought*, New York, New York, Thomas Y. Crowell Company, 1975.

Ford, Henry, and Crowther, Samuel, *Today and Tomorrow*, Garden City, New York, Doubleday, Page & Company, 1926.

Forgas, Joseph P., *Feeling and Thinking: The Role of Affect in Social Cognition*, Cambridge, United Kingdom, Cambridge University Press, 2000.

Frankl, Victor E., *Man's Search for Meaning*, New York, New York, Simon & Schuster, 1984.

Freeman, R. Edward, and Gilbert, Daniel R., *Corporate Strategy and the Search for Ethics*, Englewood Cliffs, New Jersey, Prentice Hall, 1988.

Freeman, R.E., *Strategic Management: A Stakeholder*

Appraoch, London, England, Pittman, 1984.

Frijda, Nico H., and Manstead, Anthony S. R., and Bem, Sacha, *Emotions and Belief: How Feeling Influence Thoughts*, Cambridge, United Kingdom, Cambridge University Press, 2000.

Gaarder, Jostein, *Sophie's World*, London, England, Phoenix Press, 1996.

Gardner, Howard, *Frames of Mind*, Reading, Massachusetts, Basic Books, 1983.

Gardner, Howard, *Intelligence Reframed*, Reading, Massachusetts, Basic Books, 1999.

Gardner, Howard, *Leading Minds*, Reading, Massachusetts, Basic Books, 1995.

Gardner, Howard, *Multiple Intelligences*, Reading, Massachusetts, Basic Books, 1993.

Gardner, Howard, *The Mind's New Science*, New York, New York, Basic Books, 1985.

Giarini, Orio, and Stahel, Walters, *The Limits to Certainty*, Dordrecht, The Netherlands, Kluwer Academic Publishers, 1993.

Giddins, Gary, *Visions of Jazz*, New York, New York, Oxford University Press, 1998.

Gladwell, Malcolm, *Blink: The Power of Thinking Without Thinking*, New York, New York, Little, Brown and Company, 2005.

Gladwell, Malcolm, *The Tipping Point*, London, England, Little, Brown and Company, 2000.

Goleman, Daniel, *Emotional Intellignence*, London, England, Bloomsbury Publishing, 1996.

Goold, M., and Campbell, A., *The Role of the Center in Managing Diversified Corporations*, Oxford, England, Basil Blackwell, 1987.

Grant, Michael, *The Rise of the Greeks*, London, England,

Phoenix Press, 1987.

Green, Richard, and Green, Katherine, *Inside the Dream*, New York, New York, Disney Publications, A Roundtable Press Book, 2001.

Greene, Brian, *The Elegant Universe*, London, England, Jonathan Cape, 1999.

Grover- Bolton, Dorothy, and Robert, Bolton, *People Styles at Work*, New York, New York, Amacom, 1996.

Hall, Calvin S., *Theories of Personality*, New York, New York, Wiley & Sons, 1998.

Hamel, Gary, and Prahalad, CK, *Competing for the Future*, Boston, Massachusetts, HBS Press, 1994.

Hamel, Gray, *Leading the Revolution*, Boston, Massachusetts, HBS Press, 2000.

Hansen, Valerie, *The Open Empire*, New York, New York, WW Norton & Company, 2000.

Hogarth, Robin M., *Educating Intuition*, Chicago, Illinios, University of Chicago Press, 2001.

Hume, David, *An Enquiry Concerning Human Understanding*, LaSalle, Illinios, The Open Court Publishing Company, 1958.

Hume, David, *Treatis of Human Nature*, Oxford, England, Oxford University Press, 2000.

Israel, Paul, *Edison: A Life of Invention*, New York, New York, John Wiley & Sons, 1998.

Iwerks, Leslie, and Kenworhty, John, *The Hand Behind the Mouse*, New York, New York, Disney Publications, A Roundtable Press Book, 2001.

Jacobi, Jolande, *Complex Archetype Symbol in the Psychology of CG Jung*, Princeton, New Jersey, Princeton University Press, 1959.

Jelink, M., *Institutionalizing Innovation: A Study of Organizational Learning Systems*, New York, New York,

Prager, 1979.

Jung, CG, *Modern Man in Search of A Soul*, Orlando, Florida, Harcourt, Brace and Company, 1933.

Jung, CG, *Psychological Types*, Princeton, New Jersey, Princeton University Press, 1971.

Kagan, Jerome, *Galen's Prophecy: Temperament in Human Nature*, New York, New York, Basic Books, 1994.

Kahn, Ashley, *Kind of Blue*, New York, New York, Da Capo Press, 2001.

Katzenbach, Jon R., *Peak Performance: Aligning the Hearts and Minds of Your Employees*, Boston, Massachusetts, Harvard Business School Press, 2000.

Keirsey, David, *Please Understand Me II*, Del Mar, California, Prometheus Nemesis Book Company, 1998.

Koestler, Arthur, *The Act of Creation*, London, England, Penguin Books, 1964.

Krebs-Hirsh, Sandra, and Kise, Jane AG, *Work it Out*, Palo Alto, California, Davis-Black Publishing, 1996.

Lacey, Robert, *Ford: The Men and The Machine*, Boston, Massachusetts, Little, Brown and Company, 1986.

Laird, John, *Knowledge, Belief, and Opinion*, New York, New York, The Century Company, 1930.

Lazarus, Richard S., *Emotion and Adaptation*, New York, New York, Oxford University Press, 1991.

Lazarus, Richard S., and Lazarus, Bernice, *Passion and Reason*, New York, New York, Oxford University Press, 1994.

Leary, Mark R., and Tangney, June Price, *Handbook of Self and Identity*, New York, New York, The Guilford Press, 2003.

LeDoux, Joseph, *Synaptic Self: How Our Brains Become Who We Are*, Harmondsworth, Middlesex, England, Viking: The Penguin Group, 2002.

LeDoux, Joseph, *The Emotional Brain*, New York, New York,

Touchstone: Simon & Schuster, 1996.

Lewis, Michael, and Haviland, Jeannette M., *Handbook of Emotions*, New York, New York, The Guilford Press, 1993.

Lindblom, C.E., *The Policy-Making Process*, Englewood Cliffs, New Jersey, Prentice Hall, 1968.

Lipton, Mark, *Guiding Growth: How Vision Keeps Companies on Course*, Boston, Massachusetts, Harvard Business School Press, 2003.

March, J.G., and Simon, H.A., *Organizations*, New York, New York, John Wiley & Sons, 1958.

McCaskey, Michael B., *The Executive Challenge: Managing Change and Ambiguity*, Marshfield, Massachusetts, Pittman, 1982.

McCormick, Blaine, *At Work With Thomas Edison*, Canada, Entreprenuer Press, 2001.

McKenzie, Richard B., *Trust on Trial*, Cambridge, Massachusetts, Perseus Publishing, 2000.

Miles, R.E., and Snow, C.C., *Organizational Strategy, Structure and Process*, New York, New York, MacGraw-Hill Publishing, 1978.

Miller, D., *Evolution and Revolution: A Quantum View of Structural Change in Organizations*, , Journal of Management Studies, 1982.

Mintzberg, Henry, *Strategy Formation: Schools of Thought*, New York, New York, Harper Business, 1990.

Mintzberg, Henry, and Ahlstrand, Bruce, and Lampel, Joseph, *Strategy Safari*, New York, New York, The Free Press, 1998.

Mintzberg, Henry, *The Rise and Fall of Strategic Planning*, New York, New York, The Free Press, 1994.

Mintzberg, Henry, *The Structuring of Organizations: A Synthesis of the Research*, Englewood Cliffs, New Jersey, Prentice Hall, 1979.

Moser, Paul K., *Empirical Knowledge*, Lanham, Maryland, Rowman & Littlefield Publishers, 1996.

Mosley, Leonard, *Disney's World*, Lanham, Maryland, First Scarborough House, 1990.

Mwaipaya, Paul A., *The Foundation of Hume's Philosophy*, Ashgate, Hants, England, Ashgate Publishing Ltd, 1999.

Nasi, J., *Arenas of Strategic Thinking*, Helsinki, Finland, Foundation for Economic Education, 1991.

Nonaka, I., and Takeuchi, H., *The Knowledge-Creating Company*, New York, New York, Oxford University Press, 1995.

Ohmae, Kenichi, *The Mind of the Strategist*, New York, New York, MacGraw-Hill Publishing, 1982.

Packard, David, *The HP Way: How Bill Hewlett and I Built Our Company*, New York, New York, HarperCollins Publishers, Inc., 1995.

Panskepp, Jaak, *Affective Neuroscience: The Foundations of Human and Animal Emotions*, New York, New York, Oxford University Press, 1998.

Pearson, Carol S., *Awakening the Heroes Within*, San Francisco, CA, HarperCollins Publishers, Inc., 1991.

Perkins, David, *Archimedes' Bathtub*, New York, New York, WW Norton & Company, 2000.

Pfeffer, J., and Salancik, G.R., *The External Control of Organizations:A Resource Dependence Perspective*, New York, New York, Harper & Row, 1978.

Pinker, Steven, *How the Mind Works*, New York, New York, WW Norton & Company, 1997.

Porter, Michael E, *Competitve Advantage*, New York, New York, The Free Press, 1985.

Porter, Michael E, *Competitve Strategy*, New York, New York, The Free Press, 1980.

Quinn, Robert E., *Change the World: How Ordinary People*

Can Achieve Extraordinary Results, San Francisco, CA, Jossey-Bass, 2000.

Quinn, J.B., *Strategies for Change: Logical Incrementalism*, Homewood, IL, Irwin, 1980.

Radnitsky, Gerard, and Bartley, W.W., *Evolutionary Epistemology, Rationality, and the Sociology of Knowledge*, Peru, Illinois, Open Court Publishing Company, 1993.

Rasiel, Ethan M, *The McKinsey Way*, New York, New York, MacGraw-Hill Publishing, 1999.

Rhenman, Eric, *Organization Theory for Longe-range Planning*, London, England, John Wiley & Sons, 1973.

Roback, Dr. A. A., *The Psychology of Character*, New York, New York, Harcourt, Brace and Company, 1931.

Robert, Michael, *Strategy Pure & Simple II*, New York, New York, MacGraw-Hill Publishing, 1997.

Sayre, Kenneth Malcolm, *Belief and Knowledge*, Lanham, Maryland, Rowman & Littlefield, 1997.

Schacter, Daniel L., and Scarry, Elaine, *Memory, Brain, and Belief*, Cambridge, Massachusetts, Harvard University Press, 1999.

Schein, Edgar H., *Organizational Culture and Leadership*, San Francisco, CA, Jossey-Bass, 2004.

Schendel, D.E., and Hofer, C.H., *Strategic Management: A New View of Business Policy and Planning*, Boston, Massachusetts, Little, Brown and Company, 1979.

Schumpeter, J.A., *Capitalism, Socialism and Democracy*, New York, New York, Harper & Row, 1950.

Segal, Morley, *Points of Influence: A Guide to Using Personality Theory at Work*, San Francisco, CA, Jossey-Bass, 1997.

Selznick, P., *Leadership in Administration: A Sociologic Intrepretation*, Evanston, IL, Row, Peterson, 1957.

Senge, Peter M, *The Fifth Discipline*, London, England, Century Business , 1990.

Simon, Herbert A., *Administrative Behaviour*, New York, New York, Macmillian, 1947.

Simon, Herbert A., *The New Science of Management Decision*, Englewood Cliffs, New Jersey, Prentice Hall, 1960.

Smith, Ken, and Johnson, Phil, *Business Ethics and Business Behaviour*, London, England, Thomson Business Press, 1996.

Soltis, Kenneth, *Philosophy and Education*, Chicago, Illinios, The University of Chicago Press, 1981.

Steiner, George A., *Strategic Planning*, New York, New York, The Free Press, 1997.

Steiner, George A., *Top Management Planning*, New York, New York, Macmillian, 1969.

Sternberg, Robert J., *Handbook of Intelligence*, Cambridge, United Kingdom, Cambridge University Press, 2000.

Sternberg, Robert J., *Successful Intelligence*, New York, New York, Plume, 1997.

Sternberg, Robert J., and Davidson, Janet E., *The Nature of Insight*, Boston, Massachusetts, MIT Press, 1995.

Teece, D.J., *Contributions and Impediments of Economic Analysis to the Study of Strategic Management*, New York, New York, Harper Business, 1990.

Thomas, Bob, *Building A Company*, New York, New York, Hyperion Pulishing, 1998.

Thomson, Lenore, *Personality Type: An Owner's Manual*, Boston, Massachusetts, Shambhala Publications, 1998.

Tieger, Paul D, and Barron-Tieger, Barbara, *Do What You Are*, Boston, Massachusetts, Little, Brown and Company, 1992.

Tracey, Michael, and Wiersema, Fred, *The Discipline of Market Leaders*, Reading, Massachusetts, Perseus Books, 1995.

Tregoe, Benjamin B, and Zimmerman, John W, *Top*

Management Strategy, New York, New York, Simon & Schuster, 1980.

van Fraassen, Bas C., *The Emprical Stance*, New Haven, Connecticut, Yale University Press, 2002.

Von Eckhardt, Barbara, *What is Cognitive Science?*, Cambridge, Massachusetts, MIT Press, 1993.

von Ghyczy, Tihan, and von Oetinger, Bolko, and Bassford, Christopher, *Clausewitz on Strategy*, New York, New York, John Wiley & Sons, 2001.

Weick, Karl E., *Sensemaking in Organizations*, Thousand Oaks, California, Sage Publications, 1995.

Weick, Karl E., *The Social Psychology of Organizing*, Reading, Massachusetts, Addison-Wesley, 1969.

Weick, Karl E., *The Sociology of Organizing*, Reading, Massachusetts, Addison-Wesley, 1969.

William, James, *The Will to Believe and Other Essays in Popular Philosophy*, London, England, Longmans, Green and Company, 1931.

Zeller, Eduard, *Outlines of the History of Greek Philosophy*, Bristol, England, Thoemmes Press, 1997.

TITLED PARTS OF BOOKS LISTED ALPHABETICALLY

Banaji, Mahzarin R., and Bhaskar, R. "Implicit Stereotypes and Memory: The Bounded Rationality of Social Beliefs." In *Memory, Brain, and Belief,* ed. Daniel L. Schacter and Elaine Scarry, 139-175. Cambridge: Harvard University Press, 2001.

Blascovich, Jim, and Wendy, Berry Mendes. "Challenge and Threat Appraisals: The Role of Affective Clues." In *Feeling and Thinking: The Role of Affect in Social Cognition,* ed. Joseph P. Forgas, 59-82. Cambridge: Cambridge University Press, 2000.

Clark, Lee Anna, and Watson, David. "Temperament: A New Paradigm for Trait Psychology." In *Handbook of Personality: Theory and Research,* ed. Lawrence A. Pervin, Oliver P. John, 399-419. New York: The Guilford Press, 1999.

Clore, Gerald L. "Cognition in Emotion: Always, Sometimes, or Never?" In *Cognitive Neuroscience of Emotion,* ed. Richard D. Lane and Lynn Nadel, 24-61. New York: Oxford University Press, 2000.

Clore, Gerald L., and Gasper, Karen. "Feeling is Believing: Some Affective Influences on Belief." In *Emotions and Belief,* ed. Nico H. Frijda, Antony S. R. Manstead, and Sacha Bem, 10-44. Cambridge: Cambridge University Press, 2000.

Clore, Gerald C. "Why Emotions Are Felt." In *The Nature of Emotion,* ed. Paul Ekman and Richard J. Davidson, 103-111. Oxford: Oxford University Press, 1994.

Clore, Gerald L. "Why Emotions Vary in Intensity." In Ekman, 386-393

Damasio, Antonio. "A Second Chance for Emotions." In Lane.

Damasio, Antonio. "Thinking about Belief: Concluding Remarks." In Schacter, 325-333.

Davidson, Richard J. "On Emotion, Mood, and Related Affective Constructs." In Ekman.

Ekman, Paul. "All Emotions Are Basic." In Ekman, 15-19.

Ekman, Paul, and Davidson, Richard J. "Afterword: How Do Individuals Differ in Emotion-Related Activity?" In Ekman, 342-343.

Forgas, Joseph P. "Feeling is Believing? The Role of Processing Strategies in Mediating Affective Influences on Beliefs." In Frijda, 108-143.

Frijda, Nico H., and Mesquita, Batja. "Beliefs Through Emotions." In Frijda, 45-77.

Frijda, Nico H. "Emotions Are Functional Most The Time." In

Ekman, 112-122.

Frijda, Nico H., Manstead, Anthony S. R., and Bem, Sacha. "The Influence of Emotions on Beliefs." In Frijda, 1-9.

Goldsmith, H. H. "Parsing the Emotional Domain from a Developmental Perspective." In Ekman, 68-73.

Harmon-Jones, Eddie. "A Cognitive Dissonance Theory Perspective on the Role of Emotion in the Maintenance and Change of Beliefs and Attitudes." In Frijda, 185-211.

Kihlstrom, John F. "The Psychological Unconscious." In Pervin, 424-438.

LeDoux, Joseph. "Cognitive-Emotional Interactions: Listen to the Brain." In Lane, 129-149.

LeDoux, Joseph. "Emotional Experience is an Output of, Not a Cause of Emotional Processing." In Ekman, 394-395.

Levenson, Robert W. "Human Emotion: A Functional View." In Ekman, 123-126.

Panksepp, Jaak,. "The Basics of Basic Emotion." In Ekman, 20-24.

Pickering, Alan D., and Gray, Jeffrey A. "The Neuroscience of Personality." In Pervin, 277-296.

Robins, Richard W., Norem, Julie K., and Cheek, Jonathan M. "Naturalizing the Self." In Pervin, 443-468.

Shweder, Richard A. ""You're Not Sick, You're Just in Love": Emotion as an Intrepretive System." In Ekman, 32-44.

Solomon, Robert C. "The Philosophy of Emotions." In *Handbook of Emotions,* ed. Michael Lewis and Jeannette M. Haviland, 3-15. New York: The Guilford Press, 1993.

Sparrow, Paul. "Strategic Mangement in a World Turned Upside Down: The Role of Cognition, Intuition, and Emotional Intelligence." In *Managing Strategic Implementation,* ed. Patrick Flood, 15-28. Oxford: Blackwell Publishers Ltd., 2000.

Westbury, Chris, and Dennett, Daniel C. "Mining the Past

to Construct the Future: Memory and Belief as Forms of Knowledge." In Schacter, 11-34.

Winter, David G., and Barenbaum, Nicole B. "History of Modern Personality Theory and Research." In Pervin, 3-20.

Zajonc, Robert B. "Feeling and Thinking: Closing the Debate Over the Independence of Affect." In Forgas, 31-57.

JOURNALS LISTED ALPHABETICALLY

Adelson, Rachel. "Dopamine and Desire." *Monitor on Psychology.* 36, 3 (2005): 18.

Ansoff, H.I. "Critque of Henry Mintzberg's The Design School." *Strategic Management Journal.* 12 (1991): 449-461.

Astley, W.G. "Toward an Appreciation of Collective Strategy." *Academy of Management Review.* 9, 3 (1984): 526-533.

Beinhocker, Eric D. "On the Origin of Strategies." *McKinsey Quarterly.* 4 (1999): 167-178.

Beinhocker, Eric D. "Strategy at the Edge of Chaos." *McKinsey Quarterly.* 1 (1997): 109-118.

Canli, Turhan, and Zhao, Zuo, and Gross, James. "An fMRI Study of Personality Influences on Brain Reactivity to Emotional Stimuli." *Behavorial Neuorscience.* 115, 1 (Feb-01): 33-42.

Chinn, Clark A., and Samarapungavan, Ala. "Distinguishing Between Understanding and Belief." *Theory into Practice.* 40, 4 (2001): 235-241.

Dolan, R. J. "Emotion, Cognition, and Behavior." *Science.* 298, November (2002): 1191-1194.

Drucker, Peter. "Entrepreneurship in Business Enterprise." *Journal of Business Policy.* I, 1 (1970)

Drucker, Peter. "The Theory of the Business." *Harvard Business Review.* September (1994): 95-104.

Dutton, Jane E., and Dukerich, Janet M. "Keeping an Eye on the

Mirror: Image and Identity in Organizatonal Adaptation." *The Academy of Management Journal.* 34, 3 (1991): 517-554.

Eccles, Jacquelynne S., and Wigfield, Allan. "Motivatonal Beliefs, Values, and Goals." *Annual Review Psychology.* 53 (2002): 109-132.

Feldman, S.P. "Management in Context: An Essay on the Relevance of Culture to the University of Organizational Change." *Journal of Management Studies.* 23, 6 (1986): 587-607.

Frijda, Nico H., Kuipers, Peter, and Schure, Elisabeth. "Relations Among Emotion, Appraisal, and Emotion Action Readiness." *Journal of Personality and Social Psychology.* 57, 2 (1989): 212-228.

Gluck, F.W., Kaufman, S.P., and Walleck, A.S. "Strategic Management for Competitive Advantage." *Harvard Business Review.* 58, 4 (1980): 154-161.

Goold, M. "Design, Learning and Planning: A further Observation on the Design School Debate." *Strategic Management Journal.* 13 (1992): 169-170.

Hannan, M.T., and Freeman, J. "The Population Ecology of Organizations." *American Journal of Sociology.* 82, 5 (1977): 929-964.

Harrison, Roger. "Understanding Your Organization's Character." *Harvard Business Review.* 50 May (1972): 119-128.

Lindblom, C.E. "The Science of Muddling Through." *Public Administration Review.* 19, 2 (1959): 79-88.

Marshall, Douglass. "Behavior, Belonging, and Belief: A Theory of Ritual Practice." *Sociological Theory.* 20, 3 (25-Jun-09)

Mascarenhas, Braince, and Baveja, Alok, and Jamil, Mamnoon. "Dynamics of Core Competencies in Leading Multinational Companies." *California Management Review.* 40, 4 (1998):

117-132.

Miles, R.E., and Snow, C.C., and Meyer, A.D. "Organizational Strategy, Structure and Process." *American Management Review.* July (1978): 546-562.

Miller, D. "Configurtaions Revisted." *Strategic Management Journal.* 17 (1996): 505-512.

Mintzberg, Henry. "Learning 1, Planning 0:Reply to Igor Ansoff." *Strategic Management Journal.* 12 (1991): 463-466.

Mintzberg, Henry. "Patterns of Strategy Formation." *Management Science.* (1978): 934-948.

Mintzberg, Henry. "The Design School: Reconsidering the Basic Premise of Strategic Management." *Strategic Management Journal.* 11 (1990): 171-195.

Moore, James. "Predators and Prey: A New Ecology of Competition." *Harvard Business Review.* June (1993): 76-86.

Morris, William T. "Intuition and Relevance." *Management Science.* 2, 13 (1967): 157-165.

Nasi, J. "Tracking Strategy in an Entrepreneurial Firm." *Academy of Management Journal.* 25, 3 (1982): 465-499.

Porac, Joseph F., and Thomas, Howard. "Competitive Groups as Cogntive Communities: The Case of Scottish Knitwear Manufacturers." *Journal of Management Studies.* 26, 4 (1989): 397-416.

Porter, Michael E. "Towards a Dynamic Theory of Strategy." *Strategic Management Journal.* 12 (1991): 95-117.

Prahalad, C.K., and Hamel, Gary. "The Core Competence of the Corporation." *Harvard Business Review.* 68, 3 (1990): 79-91.

Pugh, D.S., and Hickson, D.J., and Hinings, C.R. "Dimensions of Organizational Structure." *Administrative Science Quarterly.* 13 (1968): 65-105.

Reger, Rhonda K., Gustafson, Loren T., Demarie, Samuel M, and Mullane, John V. "Reframing the Organization: Why Implementing Total Quality is Easier Said Than Done." *Academy of Management Review.* 19, 3 (1994): 565-584.

Schumpeter, J.A. "The Creative Response in Economic History." *Journal of Economic History.* November (1947): 149-159.

Schwenk, Charles R. "The Cognitive Perspective on Strategic Decision-making." *Journal of Management Science.* 25, 1 (1988): 41-53.

Simon, H.A. "Making Management Decisions: The Role of Intuition and Emotion." *Academy of Mangement Executives.* 1 (1987): 57-64.

Smircich,Linda,andStubbart,Charles."StrategicManagement in an Enacted World." *The Academy of Management Review.* 10, 4 (1985): 724-736.

Synder, Allan W. "Breaking Mindset." *Mind & Language.* 13 (1998): 1-10.

Tversky, Amos, and Kahneman, Daniel. "Availability: A Heuristic for Judging Frequency and Probability." *Cognitive Psychology.* 5 (1973): 207-232.

Williams, Allan O. "A Belief-Focused Process Model of Organizational Learning." *Journal of Management Studies.* 38, 1 (2001): 67-85.

Wylie, Mary Sykes, and Simon, Richard. "Discoveries from the Black Box." *Pscyhotherapy Networker.* 26, 5 (2002): 1-12.

MAGAZINES

Cose, Ellis. "From Schools to Jobs, Black Women Are Rising Much Faster Than Black Men." *Newsweek.* February 23. 2003.

Guterl, Fred. "What Freud Got Right." *Newsweek.* November

11, 2002, 50.

Roberts, Johnnie. "The New Black Power." *Newsweek.* January 20 2002

"The New Breed of Strategic Planner." *Business Week.* 17-Sep-84, 62-68.

ONLINE MAGAZINES

Marano, Hara Estroff. "The Psychic Cinema: The Real Reason Why We Dream." *Pscyhology Today Magazine.* March 2005, http://www.neuropsa.org.uk/downloads/PsychCinemaPsychToday05.doc

NEWSPAPERS

Begley, Sharon. "Expectations May Alter Outcomes Far More Than We Realize." *Wall Street Journal.* November 7, 2003, B1.

Cha, Ariana Eunjung. "Hewlett-Packard Forces Celebrity CEO to Quit." *Washington Post.* February 10, 2005, A01.

WEBSITES

Bellis, Mary. "Inventors: Edward Goodrich Acheson - Inventor of Carborundum." *About, Inc. a part of the New York Times.* 2005, http://inventors.about.com/library/inventors/blacheson.htm.

Bellis, Mary. "Inventors: Scotch Tape and Richard Drew." *About, Inc. a part of the New York Times.* 2005, http://inventors.about.com/library/inventors/blscotchtape.htm.

Bellis, Mary. "Inventors: The History of the Telephone." *About, Inc. a part of the New York Times.* 2005, http://inventors.about.com/library/inventors/bltelephone.htm.

Bellis, Mary. "Inventors: The Invention of the Wheel." *About, Inc. a part of the New York Times.* 2005, http://inventors. about.com/library/inventors/blwheel.htm.

Bellis, Mary. "Inventors: The Wild History of Roller Skates or Dry Land Skating." *About, Inc. a part of the New York Times.* 2005, http://inventors.about.com/library/weekly/ aa050997.htm.

Bhattacharya, Shanoi. "Brains Drained by Hidden Race Bias." *NewScientist.com.* 17 November 17, 2003, http://www. newscientist.com/article.ns?id=dn4388(accessed October 22, 2005).

Gromov, Gregory. "History of Internet and WWW: The Crossoads of Internet History." *Gregory Gromov.* 2003, http://netvalley.com/intvalweb.html.

Jobs, Steve. ""You've got to find what you love," Jobs says." *The Stanford Report, Stanford University.* June 12, 2005, http://news-service.stanford.edu/news/2005/june15/ jobs-061505.html (accessed October 12, 2005).

Sink, Eric W. "Memoirs from the Browser Wars." *Eric.Weblog.* 2003, http://software.ericsink.com/Browser_Wars.html.

Walker, Rob. "America's 25 Most Fascinating Entrepreneurs: Jeff Bezos." *Inc.com.* April 1, 2004, http://inc.com/ magazine/20040401/25bezos.html (accessed October 12, 2005).

Young, Emma. "Rejection Massively Reduces IQ." *NewScientist. com.* March 15, 2002, http://www.newscientist.com/ article.ns?id=dn2051.

"The Blizzard of 1888. Infoplease." *Pearson Education, publishing as Infoplease.* 2005, http://www.infoplease. com/spot/blizzard1.html.

"Bridging the Urban Landscape: Neighborhoods: North Side: George Ferris." *Carnegie Library of Pittsburgh.* 2005, http://alphaclp.clpgh.org/CLP/exhibit/neighborhoods/

northside/nor%5Fn105.html.

"Inventor of the Week Archive: Edwin Herbert Land." *Massachusetts Institute of Technology.* 1996, http://web. mit.edu/invent/iow/land.html.

"InventoroftheWeekArchive:TheSkateboard."*Massachusetts Institute of Technology.* 1997, http://web.mit.edu/invent/ iow/skateboard.html.

"MediaMattersExposesBennett."*MediaMattersforAmerica.* 2005, http://mediamatters.org/items/200509280006.

"The Bill Evans Webpages." 2005, http://www. billevanswebpages.com/kindblue.html.

"The Blizzard of 1888." *The Graduate Center, City University of New York.* 2001, http://www.vny.cuny.edu/blizzard/ introduction/intro_set.html.

Permissions

Excerpts on pages 8, 10, and 11: Akio Morita, *Made in Japan: Akio Morita and Sony*, E. P. Dutton, 1986, p 46, 50, and 58. Used by permission of Dutton, a division of Penguin Group (USA) Inc.

Excerpts on pages 8 and 11: Sony Corporation, *Sony History*, http://www.sony.net/Fun/SH/

Page 9: Kobayahi Shigeru, *Creative Management*, American Management Association, 1971, p 5.

Excerpts on pages 13, 14, and 15: Nick Lyons, *The Sony Vision*, Crown Publishers, Inc., 1976, pp. 51, 109, 131, 144.

Page 21: Bob Thomas, *Building A Company: Roy O. Disney and The Creation of an Entertainment Empire*, Hyperion, 1998, p 110.

Page 33: Figure 6.5 The Anatomical Pathways Supporting Different Types of Memory and text excerpts on pp. 27, 33, 34, 41. Reprinted by permission of the publisher from MEMORY, BRAIN, AND BELIEF, edited by Daniel L. Schacter and Elaine Scarry, pp. 21, 141, 143, 195, 196, Cambridge, Mass. Harvard University Press, Copyright © 2001 by the President and Fellows of Harvard College.

Pages 38 and 108: Antonio Damasio, *Descartes' Error*, Quill, Copyright © 2000, p 173 and 188. Used by permission of G. P. Putnam's Sons, a division of Penguin Group (USA) Inc.

Page 40: Johnnie Roberts, "*The New Black Power*," Newsweek, January 20, 2002.

Page 41: Ellis Cose, "*From Schools to Jobs, Black Women Are Rising Much Faster Than Black Men*," Newsweek, February 23, 2003.

Page 45: "Media Matters Exposes Bennett," *Media Matters for America*, 2005, http://mediamatters.org/items/200509280006.

Pages 106, 194, and 195: David Perkins, *Archimedes' Bathtub*, W.W. Norton, 2000, p 131, 146, and 147. Used by permission of W. W. Norton & Company

Page 123: "Agnes Macdonald-Spirit of Service," Courtesy of Telecom Pioneers. All Rights Reserved.

Page 130: Figure 4.2: Normal Decision-making Uses Two Complementary Paths and text excerpts on pages 130 and 105. Antonio Damasio, *Looking for Spinoza*, Harcourt Books, 2003, p 93, 147, 149. Reprinted by permission of Harcourt, Inc.

Page 133: Edgar H. Schein, *Organizational Culture and Leadership*, Jossey-Bass, 2004, p 17.

Page 134: Peter F. Drucker, *Concept of the Corporation*, 1993, Introduction to the Transaction Edition. Reprinted by permission of Transaction Publishers.

Page 140: Hewlett-Packard Company, History and Facts, http://www.hp.com/hpinfo/abouthp/histnfacts/timeline/hist_50s.html.

Page 14: James C. Collins and Jerry I. Porras, *Built to Last*, HarperBusiness Essentials, 2002, p 209. Reprinted by permission of Jim Collins.

Excerpt on page 142 from STRATEGY SAFARI: A Guided Tour Through the Wilds of Strategic Management by Henry Mintzberg, Bruce Ahlstrand and Joseph Lampel. Copyright ©1998 by Henry Mintzberg, Ltd., Bruce Ahlstrand, Joseph Lampel. Reprinted with permission of The Free Press, a Division of Simon & Schuster Adult Publishing Group. All rights reserved.

Page 154: Gerald L. Clore, *Feeling is Believing: Some Affective Influences on Belief*, in Emotions and Belief, ed. Nico H. Fridja, 2000, p 26. Reprinted with the permission of Cambridge University Press.

Page 154: Karl E. Weick, Sensemaking in Organizations, Sage Publications, 1995, p 133.

Page 157: Steve Jobs, ""You've Got to Find What You Love," Jobs says," The Stanford Report, Stanford University, June 12, 2005, http://newsservice.stanford.edu/news/2005/

june15/jobs-061505.html (accessed October 12, 2005).

Text excerpts on pages 171, 172, and 173: Ashley Kahn, *Kind of Blue*, Da Capo Press, 2001, pp 7, 17, and 99. Reprinted by permission of Perseus Publishing.

Excerpts on pages 199 - 202 from *A Century of Innovation*, 3M Company, 2002.

Page 209: Joseph LeDoux, *The Emotional Brain*, Touchstone, (New York: Simon & Schuster, 1996).

Page 210: Figure 6-13: The Low and High Roads to the Amygdala. Reprinted with permission from Simon & Schuster Adult Publishing Group from THE EMOTIONAL BRAIN by Joseph LeDoux. Copyright © 1996 by Joseph LeDoux.

Pages 217: *Competing on Internet Time* by Michael A. Cusumano and David Yoffie. Copyright © 1998 Michael A. Cusumano and David Yoffie. Reprinted with permission of The Free Press, a Division of Simon & Schuster Adult Publishing Group. All rights reserved.

Page 215: Eric W. Sink, "Memoirs from the Browser Wars." Eric.Weblog. 2003, http://software.ericsink.com/Browser_Wars.html.

Page 218: Richard B. McKenzie, *Trust on Trial*, 2000, Perseus Publishing, p 21. Reprinted by permission of Perseus Publishing.

Page 238: Carol S. Pearson, *Awakening the Heroes Within*, HarperSanFrancisco, 1991, pp 10 and 11. Reprinted by permission of HarperCollins Publishers.

Every effort has been made to contact the copyright holders of each of the selections. Rights holders of any selection not credited should contact HPH Publishing, 333 W. North Ave, Ste. 289, Chicago, IL 60610, in order for a correction to be made in the next reprinting of our work.

Index